k

Access to History
General Editor: Keith Randell

Britain: Foreign and Imperial Affairs 1939-64

Alan Farmer

Hodder & Stoughton

A MEMBER OF THE HODDER HEADLINE GROUP

The cover illustration is a portrait of Winston Churchill by Frank Salisbury. (Courtesy of the National Trust Photographic Library.)

Some other titles in the series:

Britain: Foreign and Imperial Affairs 1919-39   ISBN 0 340 55928 4
Alan Farmer

Britain: Domestic Politics 1918-39   ISBN 0 340 55647 1
Robert Pearce

Britain: Industrial Relations and the Economy 1900-39   ISBN 0 340 57374 0
Robert Pearce

Labour and Reform: Working Class Movements 1815-1914   ISBN 0 340 52930 X
Clive Behagg

Italy: Liberalism and Fascism 1870-1945   ISBN 0 340 54548 8
Mark Robson

Germany: The Third Reich 1933-45   ISBN 0 340 53847 3
Geoff Layton

British Library Cataloguing in Publication Data

Farmer, Alan
    Britain: Foreign and Imperial Affairs 1939-64
    (Access to History Series)
    I. Title II. Series
    327.4100904

ISBN 0-340-59256-7

First published 1994

Impression number   10   9   8   7   6   5   4   3   2   1
Year   1998   1997   1996   1995   1994

Typeset by Sempringham publishing, Bedford
Printed in Great Britain for Hodder & Stoughton Educational, a division of Hodder Headline Plc, Mill Road, Dunton Green, Sevenoaks, Kent TN13 2YA by Page Bros (Norwich) Ltd

Contents

Preface

To the general reader

Although the *Access to History* series has been designed with the needs of students studying the subject at higher examination levels very much in mind, it also has a great deal to offer the general reader. The main body of the text (i.e. ignoring the Study Guides at the ends of chapters) forms a readable and yet stimulating survey of a coherent topic as studied by historians. However, each author's aim has not merely been to provide a clear explanation of what happened in the past (to interest and inform): it has also been assumed that most readers wish to be stimulated into thinking further about the topic and to form opinions of their own about the significance of the events that are described and discussed (to be challenged). Thus, although no prior knowledge of the topic is expected on the reader's part, she or he is treated as an intelligent and thinking person throughout. The author tends to share ideas and possibilities with the reader, rather than passing on numbers of so-called 'historical truths'.

To the student reader

There are many ways in which the series can be used by students studying History at a higher level. It will, therefore, be worthwhile thinking about your own study strategy before you start your work on this book. Obviously, your strategy will vary depending on the aim you have in mind, and the time for study that is available to you.

If, for example, you want to acquire a general overview of the topic in the shortest possible time, the following approach will probably be the most effective:

1 Read chapter 1 and think about its contents.
2 Read the 'Making notes' section at the end of chapter 2 and decide whether it is necessary for you to read this chapter.
3 If it is, read the chapter, stopping at each heading to note down the main points that have been made.
4 Repeat stage 2 (and stage 3 where appropriate) for all the other chapters.

If, however, your aim is to gain a thorough grasp of the topic, taking however much time is necessary to do so, you may benefit from carrying out the same procedure with each chapter, as follows:

1 Read the chapter as fast as you can, and preferably at one sitting.
2 Study the flow diagram at the end of the chapter, ensuring that you understand the general 'shape' of what you have just read.

3 Read the 'Making notes' section (and the 'Answering essay questions' section, if there is one) and decide what further work you need to do on the chapter. In particularly important sections of the book, this will involve reading the chapter a second time and stopping at each heading to think about (and to write a summary of) what you have just read.

4 Attempt the 'Source-based questions' section. It will sometimes be sufficient to think through your answers, but additional understanding will often be gained by forcing yourself to write them down.

When you have finished the main chapters of the book, study the 'Further Reading' section and decide what additional reading (if any) you will do on the topic.

This book has been designed to help make your studies both enjoyable and successful. If you can think of ways in which this could have been done more effectively, please write to tell me. In the meantime, I hope that you will gain greatly from your study of History.

Keith Randell

Acknowledgements

The Publishers would like to thank the following for permission to reproduce illustrations in this volume:

'Winston Churchill' by Frank Salisbury / National Trust Photographic Library - cover.
David Low, *Evening Standard* 2 March 1948 / Cartoon Study Centre, University of Kent, Canterbury p. 40.
Punch Publications p. 45.
Vicky, *News Chronicle* p. 62 top.
David Low, *Daily Herald* 12 January 1951 / Cartoon Study Centre, University of Kent, Canterbury p. 62 lower.
Vicky, *News Chronicle* 19 June 1950 / British Newspaper Library p. 69.

The Publishers would also like to thank the following for permission to reproduce copyright material:

Jonathan Cape for the extract from *Never Again*, Peter Hennessey, 1992; Extracts from *British Defence White Paper 1957* reproduced with the permission of the Controller of Her Majesty's Stationary Office; Weidenfeld and Nicolson for the extracts from *Suez*, K. Kyle, 1991.

Every effort has been made to trace and acknowledge ownership of copyright. The Publishers will be glad to make suitable arrangements with any copyright holders whom it has not been possible to contact.

CHAPTER 1

Introduction: The Framework of Policy-Making

1 Britain: 1939 and 1964

In 1939 few people had any doubts that Britain was a great power. This seemed self-evident. The British Empire amounted to nearly 25 per cent of the world's land surface and a similar proportion of its population. France, with the next largest empire (excluding the USSR), accounted for only 9 per cent of the earth's land surface. In a crisis (such as the First World War) the Empire could be a vast resource of material and manpower. There seemed little to suggest in 1939 that the Empire was near to the point of disintegration. Most Britons were proud of the Empire, seeing it as an efficient and benevolent system which brought peace, prosperity and happiness to less fortunate peoples. Most assumed that it would take decades, perhaps centuries, before most colonial territories were ready for independence. In 1939, moreover, no country actually posed an immediate threat to the Empire. Even Hitler, the Nazi dictator of Germany, wanted it to continue to exist!

The Empire was sustained by (and helped sustain) Britain's economic strength. In 1939 Britain was still the world's greatest trading nation. Her economy was strong enough to bind all the countries of the Empire to the British imperial system. Colonies and self-governing dominions relied on Britain for banking facilities, for investment, for manufactured goods and as a market for their principal exports. The introduction of imperial preference in the 1930s had further strengthened the linkage between Britain and her Empire.

Britain's economic strength meant that she had the resources to afford large armaments. The British navy continued to rule the waves. By 1939 Britain was in the throes of greatly increasing her airforce, so much so that by 1940 she would be producing more planes than Germany. The vast British-controlled Indian army was a useful force for policing far-flung imperial possessions.

Britain had European as well as imperial interests. By the late 1930s she was regarded, and saw herself, as the country best able to counter-balance the strength of Nazi Germany. In consequence Britain was concerned about the future of East European countries like Czechoslovakia and Poland.

Twenty-five years later, Britain was no longer a superpower. By 1964 the vast majority of the 80 or so territories which had made up the British Empire in 1939 had gone. Britain had been eclipsed as an economic power, not just by the USA and the USSR, but by Germany, Japan and France. Militarily Britain was not in the same league as the USA and the USSR. Indeed by 1964 she was heavily dependent upon

the USA for her defence and yet still faced the possibility of total
destruction at the hands of Russia (and had little control over American
policy which might bring about that total destruction). 'Never surely,
except under the impact of overwhelming military defeat . . . has a great
country gone so rapidly from world power to extreme helplessness',
wrote George Kennan, an American diplomat and historian.

Why, in a 25-year-period, had Britain's international position
declined so sharply? What had gone wrong?

Historians have a variety of explanations for Britain's decline.

a) Some historians are convinced that the seeds of Britain's decline
were sown well before 1939. They see Britain's position in jeopardy
pre-1914, with the retreat continuing through the 1920s and 1930s.
Some stress economic decline. Some stress a growth of moral
squeamishness among British leaders and the British public. Some
emphasise changing world circumstances and claim that the USA and
the USSR (and possibly Germany and Japan) were almost certain to
overtake Britain in the great power league table. Others believe that the
rise of nationalism within the colonies meant that the Empire's days
were numbered. Without the Empire Britain could/would no longer be a
great power. Historians of the 'writing on the wall' school are convinced
that Britain's decline was almost inevitable, whoever was in power after
1939 and whatever they did. They see the Second World War as simply
a catalyst, an accelerator of already established trends.

b) Others historians prefer to emphasise the importance of the
Second World War. They see Britain as a first rate power in 1939 and
are convinced that the Empire was not in irreversible decline. They
think the Second World War seriously weakened Britain, thus
instigating her decline. Some, therefore, have questioned Britain's
involvement in the war, arguing that the policies of appeasement
pursued by Neville Chamberlain (and others) in the 1930s made more
sense than Winston Churchill's 'gung-ho' notions.

c) Other historians blame post-war British governments. Some blame
the Labour government (1945-51) for sacrificing India, the jewel in the
crown of the British Empire, for failing to take the leading role in Europe
and/or for tying Britain too closely to the USA. Others criticise the
Conservative governments from 1951 to 1964, especially Anthony
Eden's government for the 1956 Suez debacle.

d) Other historians think Britain's decline was due more to profound
economic, social, cultural and attitudinal changes in Britain after 1945.
The British public, it is claimed, was simply not interested in the Empire
and was unwilling to see scarce resources spent on preserving it. Most
Britons were more concerned with issues of employment and social
welfare than with defence of imperial frontiers. Politicians, arguably,
simply reflected public opinion.

Britain's decline as a great power is a subject of massive complexity. It
is, moreover, a subject which arouses strong emotions. It is still hard, for

example, to look dispassionately at the career of Winston Churchill who, despite his many failings, has become a figure of almost God-like proportions. The break-up of Britain's Empire is also a controversial subject. To some the end of colonial rule is a moral victory to be celebrated. To others it is a disaster to be deplored. Perhaps the only thing that can be stated with some certainty is that no simple single causal explanation for Britain's decline will do. It is likely that pre-1939 weaknesses, the impact of the Second World War, and the actions of governments (reflecting public opinion) after 1945 all contributed to Britain's loss of great power status. The next section will examine Britain's weaknesses in 1939. The impact of the Second World War and the actions of British governments from 1939 to 1964 will form the subject matter of the rest of the book.

2 British Weakness in 1939

Most historians would accept that Britain's position in 1939 was not as strong as it might initially seem to have been or as some politicians at the time (not least Winston Churchill) imagined it to be. By 1939 Russia, Germany and France all had far larger armies than Britain. The USA and Japan had powerful navies. The USA was economically stronger than Britain. Germany produced more coal, iron and steel. Stalin's Five Year Plans had led to a great increase in Russian industrial production. The USA, Russia and Germany all had much larger populations.

The British Empire, although large, was, in reality, a hotch-potch of independent, semi-independent and dependent countries held together by economic, political or cultural links that varied greatly in strength and character. By 1931 the most developed parts of the Empire - the 'white' dominions - were effectively independent and sought to assert their independence. This meant that Britain could no longer take their support for granted. Many Afrikaaner South Africans and French Canadians had no love for Britain. The same was even more true of the southern Irish. British control of India was superficial. It very much depended on the Indians themselves, and many were growing restive. By 1939 the granting of dominion status to India seemed likely, if not inevitable. Much of the rest of the Empire was underdeveloped politically, socially and economically. British colonial policy in the inter-war years was essentially one of benevolent neglect. Given that Britain put so little in, she could expect to get little out.

Administering and defending such a heterogeneous and widely scattered collection of territories were major problems. Indeed some historians view the over-extended Empire as a strategic liability, rather than a strength. Nor were all British people convinced of the virtues of the Empire. Many on the left had doubts about the justice of British imperial rule. Arguably, therefore, Britain's long imperial career was near to being played out by 1939.

Wealth usually determines power, and Britain's declining ability to shape world affairs owed much to a diminution in her relative economic strength. By 1900 British industry faced strong competition from Germany and the USA. During the 1920s and 1930s historians have seen Britain suffering from a variety of economic ills - poor management, outdated technology, poor salesmanship, a low rate of investment, overpowerful trade unions and shoddy workmanship. In the late 1930s Britain started to have a persistent balance of payments deficit, reflecting its weakening industrial position.

Economic difficulties reduced Britain's capacity to increase her armaments. By the 1930s British seapower, vital for the defence of the Empire, was overstretched as Britain faced naval challenges from the USA, Japan and Italy. Moreover naval power was no longer sufficient to defend Britain herself. During the First World War German submarines had threatened to starve Britain into surrender. More serious still were aircraft developments. Enemy bombers could now leap-frog the English Channel. Britain was no longer safe from attack. London, the centre of government and home for one fifth of Britain's population, was probably a more significant target than anywhere else in Europe.

In the 1930s Britain was threatened by the growing strength and ambitions of Germany, Italy, Japan and Russia. Hitler planned to control Central and Eastern Europe and it was impossible to know where exactly his ambition would stop. Mussolini, the Fascist leader of Italy, hoped to make the Mediterranean Sea an Italian lake. This was a direct challenge to Britain which had controlled the Mediterranean for over a century. Japan's expansionist dreams seemed a potential threat to Britain's possessions in Asia. Some, especially on the right, considered communist Russia a threat to world peace and stability.

Government critics in the 1930s, both on the left and right, demanded that Britain should play a tough world policeman role, taking on aggressors wherever they appeared. The left thought Britain should do this via the League of Nations, believing that the League would somehow preserve peace without a special effort on anyone's part. Many on the left called for action against Germany, Italy and Japan and yet supported British disarmament. They naively imagined that somehow 'moral' force and the threat of sanctions would be sufficient to stop Hitler, Mussolini and/or the Japanese militarists.

The right appreciated the importance of force but tended to overestimate Britain's strength. Churchill, for example, believed that Britain could and should have stopped Hitler and the other aggressors sooner. It is often forgotten that, in all probability, this would not have avoided war. Churchill's war - or wars - would simply have been fought sooner rather than later and it is far from certain that this would have been to Britain's advantage.

Historians have tended to follow Churchill and blame the 'appeasers' of the 1930s, especially Neville Chamberlain, for pursuing conciliatory policies. But some recent historians have treated the 1930s British governments with more sympathy, stressing the horrendous problems they faced, and claiming that they were far more realistic than their critics. British governments accepted that there was a growing disparity between Britain's world-wide commitments and her capacity to meet them. They realised that Britain's only certain ally was France, a country which was politically and socially divided. They acknowledged, for most of the 1930s, that certain parts of the world were outside Britain's domain. The Chiefs of Staff stressed repeatedly that Britain was incapable of defying Germany, Italy and Japan simultaneously. Aware that the British economy could not withstand the impact of a long war and that Britain could not militarily win a short war, British statesmen sensibly did their best to avoid conflict.

3 Who Made British Foreign Policy?

In the making of British external policy, the relationship between Prime Minister and Foreign Secretary was (and still is) crucial. The relative power and influence of Foreign Secretaries in relation to Prime Ministers varied according to the personalities involved. Some Prime Ministers chose Foreign Secretaries whom they could trust and to whom they felt able to delegate substantial authority. Others tried to run their own foreign policies, sometimes coming into conflict with their Foreign Secretaries. Of all the Foreign Secretaries who held office in the period 1939-64 only two, Ernest Bevin and Anthony Eden, took significant personal initiatives. Responsibility in the main rested with the Prime Minister.

The shaping of British policy did not totally depend on the decisions of Prime Ministers and Foreign Secretaries. All Prime Ministers had to consider the views of other members of the Cabinet. Relatively few diplomatic or 'imperial' issues actually reached Cabinet level and when they did most Prime Ministers were able to have the last word. Nevertheless, all Prime Ministers realised the necessity of having the support of the Cabinet on key foreign issues and even strong Prime Ministers heeded the advice of their Cabinets, sometimes against their better judgement.

Prime Ministers and their Cabinets were ultimately responsible to Parliament. Although Parliament rarely intervened in day-to-day foreign affairs, many individual MPs were very interested in external developments and often questioned the wisdom of government policy. In the last resort Parliament could force governments to take particular courses of action. For example, given the feeling in the House of Commons, Neville Chamberlain would have found it impossible not to have declared war on Germany on 3 September 1939.

Parliament, in turn, represented public opinion. Although the public as a whole was rarely interested in the details of external policy, public opinion could not be ignored and set the broad ideological framework within which governments had to operate. The fact that most people preferred governments in peacetime to spend money on domestic matters rather than on defence and adventures abroad was something that governments, anxious to win elections, could not ignore.

The public, in turn, were influenced by the mass media, particularly by the press but increasingly by radio, newsreels (which people saw when they went to the cinema) and by television (from the mid-1950s). To what extent the media were influenced by - or influenced - both governments and public opinion is keenly debated by historians. Certainly the media were in a position to shape the agenda of public debate by focusing on certain news items and giving them particular colouring and significance. Developments in communication meant that statesmen now negotiated in the full glare of publicity. However, governments have invariably found ways of managing the media. The press, for example, was persuaded to conceal the news of Churchill's stroke in 1953 and the fact that Britain was run without him for a month!

Arguably external policy-making was as much in the hands of professional civil servants in the Foreign Office as politicians. The most senior Foreign Office civil servant, the Permanent Under-Secretary, was in a strong position to exert influence on Foreign Secretaries and thus determine overall policy. However, other Whitehall departments also had some control over overseas policy. In the imperial sphere the dominant force before 1947 was the India Office, linking Whitehall with the Indian sub-continent via a Viceroy who had substantial authority. The Colonial Office dealt with Britain's other overseas territories. There was also a Dominions Office to handle relations with Canada, Newfoundland, Australia, New Zealand, South Africa and the Irish Free State. After Indian independence in 1947 the Indian and Dominion Offices were merged to form the Commonwealth Relations Office. Treasury officials, because they were in a position to scrutinise all proposals involving government spending, also had considerable power. Foreign policy, therefore, was handled by a plethora of (often rival) civil service departments. The harmonizing of different and often conflicting viewpoints swallowed up time and energies. The lack of effective machinery for policy review was particularly serious. A formal planning unit was not established until 1957. Before 1964 there was not even a daily conference of senior officials.

Some historians are convinced that the civil servants provided devoted and competent service. But others think that the existence of an entrenched civil service bureaucracy resulted in lower-common-denominator policies which satisfied most interests to some degree but which may have prevented radical changes of policy. Many of the senior civil servants came from similar backgrounds to the politicians. They attended the same public schools (especially Eton and Harrow), the same universities (overwhelmingly Oxford and Cambridge) and often

Government	Prime Minister	Foreign Secretary
May 1937 National Conservative	Neville Chamberlain	Anthony Eden (Feb. 1938 Lord Halifax)
May 1940 Coalition	Winston Churchill	Lord Halifax (Dec. 1940 Anthony Eden)
May 1945 Caretaker	Winston Churchill	Anthony Eden
July 1945 Labour	Clement Attlee	Ernest Bevin
February 1950 Labour	Clement Attlee	Ernest Bevin (Mar. 1951 Herbert Morrison)
October 1951 Conservative	Winston Churchill	Anthony Eden
April 1955 Conservative	Anthony Eden	Harold Macmillan (Dec. 1955 Selwyn Lloyd)
January 1957 Conservative	Harold Macmillan	Selwyn Lloyd (July 1960 Lord Home)
October 1963 Conservative	Sir Alec Douglas-Home (Formerly Lord Home)	R.A. Butler
October 1964 Labour	Harold Wilson	P. Gordon Walker

frequented the same London clubs. It has been claimed that this 'elite' controlled policy in their own 'class' interests. This conclusion is perhaps too sweeping. It certainly does not account for the fact that members of this elite had very different views on many policy issues.

The final - and obvious - point is that British policy was largely determined by the actions of non-Britons. As Herbert Morrison, Labour Foreign Secretary in 1951, put it, 'Foreign Policy would be O.K. except for the bloody foreigners'. British Prime Ministers, Foreign Secretaries, Cabinets, Parliaments, public opinion, media or civil servants had little control over the policies of the USA, Russia, Germany, Japan etc and British policy-makers had, of necessity, to respond to the actions of a variety of powers, both friendly and hostile.

For most of the period 1939-64, Prime Ministers, Foreign Secretaries and Cabinet took the essential decisions. Leading politicians, however, usually gave the impression that they were more in control of events than was the case. In reality government decisions were often knee-jerk reactions to surprise crises and were often taken on the basis of poor information and in the context of a mass of conflicting problems.

4 British Foreign and Imperial Policy pre-1939

This book is concerned with British foreign and imperial policy between 1939 and 1964. However, some understanding of the main aims of external policy-makers in the 1920s and 1930s is essential in terms of understanding British policy-making after 1939. Although there were differences of emphasis, most inter-war governments, whether Conservative, Labour or National, tended to pursue similar aims. The maintenance of peace seemed Britain's greatest national interest. The terrible losses of the First World War made both politicians and public recoil from the prospect of a new war. Peace helped promote commerce, essential to prosperity. There was also an awareness that Britain was vulnerable to air attack. By the 1930s Britain seemed to have everything to lose and little to gain from a major war.

Although governments did their best to avoid conflict, most were also concerned to ensure that, if war should come, Britain was adequately defended. British defence policy was based on four main objectives: the security of the United Kingdom; the protection of essential trade routes; defence of the Empire; and a readiness to co-operate in the defence of Britain's allies. Governments had to assess Britain's defence requirements in the light of the international situation and in terms of what the country could afford. Until the mid 1930s successive governments tried to keep defence spending as low as possible, and to promote disarmament whenever they could.

It had long been recognised that allies could enhance Britain's strength. Many politicians hoped for a closer co-operation with the USA, potentially the world's greatest power. Without American help it was unlikely that Britain and France would have won the First World War. But after 1919 the USA was reluctant to involve herself in European, or indeed world, affairs. Although President Franklin D. Roosevelt was not indifferent to Europe (or Asia), his willingness and ability to act was severely constrained by the political and economic situation within the USA. British governments soon realised they could not base their foreign policy upon the expectation of American support. Throughout the inter-war years Britain's main ally was France. But British and French interests were far from being identical and there were times when the two countries were at odds. The increasing power of Nazi Germany, however, concerned both countries and encouraged increased co-operation.

British interests were global rather than just continental and few politicians considered Britain a fully European state. However, most appreciated the importance of Europe to Britain. All governments hoped to maintain some kind of European balance of power as the best insurance against the renewal of war. But most were also reluctant to assume any definite commitments in the furtherance of this aim.

Membership of a Continental military alliance might well force Britain to maintain a larger army than she could afford.

In the late 1930s Adolf Hitler, bent on gobbling territory in Central and Eastern Europe, seemed to threaten the balance of power in Europe. Some politicians (notably Winston Churchill) argued that Britain should stand up to Hitler. British governments, however, fearing Italian and Japanese involvement, and wary of Stalin's Russia which was likely to be the only country to benefit from a British/French - German conflict preferred negotiation. Since the Second World War appeasement has tended to have a derogatory meaning, and the word is often used to mean a craven surrender to force. But for most of the 1930s appeasement was viewed positively: the continuation of a long diplomatic tradition of trying to settle disputes peacefully. Those who opposed appeasement were seen as war-mongers. Only the failure of Chamberlain's policies in 1939 (when he actually abandoned appeasement!) turned appeasement into a pejorative term.

In September 1939 Britain went to war with Nazi Germany as a result of a quarrel between Germany and Poland over Danzig and the Polish Corridor. Since 1939 most historians have argued that Britain was right to declare war on Germany. However some historians have recently questioned the wisdom of this step. By allying with Poland, Britain certainly broke one of the cardinal tenets of her foreign policy: no commitments in Eastern Europe. British military chiefs were aware that there was no way that Britain could actually help Poland - a country with a corrupt, elitist and racist government which had been allied with Hitler throughout the 1930s. It might have been in Britain's best interests to have encouraged Hitler to keep pressing eastwards (away from Britain) so that he would come up against the USSR. But this can only be conjecture. The reality - in September 1939 - was that Britain was at war with Germany; a war which Britain could not really afford to fight but a war which she could certainly not afford to lose.

Working on 'Introduction: The Framework of Policy-Making'

The chapter has four objectives: to give you an understanding of Britain's strengths and weaknesses in 1939; to make you aware that historians have different views about Britain's position in 1939 and the impact of the Second World War; to give you some notion of how British policy was made; and to provide you with some understanding of British foreign policy pre-1939. You do not need to make very detailed notes but you do need to have some grasp of these areas before tackling the rest of the book. As you read the following chapters, you must try and judge why Britain declined as a great power. Was decline inevitable or were particular (or all) British governments to blame?

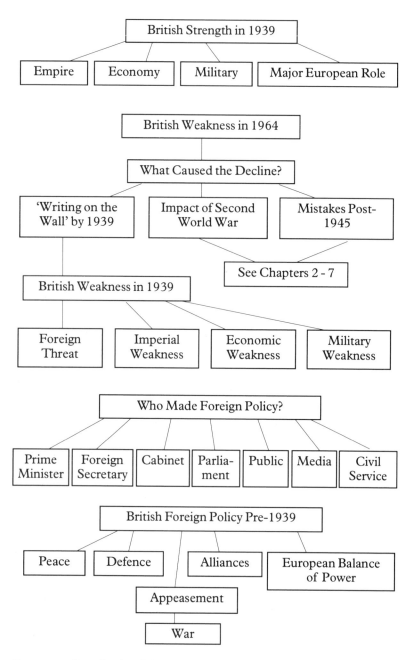

```
                    ┌──────────────────────────┐
                    │  British Strength in 1939 │
                    └──────────────────────────┘
   ┌─────────┐   ┌──────────┐   ┌──────────┐   ┌─────────────────────┐
   │ Empire  │   │ Economy  │   │ Military │   │ Major European Role │
   └─────────┘   └──────────┘   └──────────┘   └─────────────────────┘
```

British Strength in 1939

Empire   Economy   Military   Major European Role

British Weakness in 1964

What Caused the Decline?

'Writing on the Wall' by 1939   Impact of Second World War   Mistakes Post-1945

See Chapters 2 - 7

British Weakness in 1939

Foreign Threat   Imperial Weakness   Economic Weakness   Military Weakness

Who Made Foreign Policy?

Prime Minister   Foreign Secretary   Cabinet   Parliament   Public   Media   Civil Service

British Foreign Policy Pre-1939

Peace   Defence   Alliances   European Balance of Power

Appeasement

War

Summary - Introduction: The Framework of Policy-Making

CHAPTER 2

The Second World War

1 From Chamberlain to Churchill

In September 1939 Neville Chamberlain, who for two years had attempted to keep peace, found himself leading a nation at war. He wrote in his diary how, 'I hate and loathe this war. I was never meant to be a War Minister'. But his iron sense of duty, and a natural reluctance to step down from the premiership, kept him in office. As proof of his determination to wage war to the best of his ability, Chamberlain reformed his government, bringing in Winston Churchill as First Lord of the Admiralty and Anthony Eden as Dominion Secretary.

While Britain prepared for war, Germany struck at Poland. Using tanks and aircraft to considerable effect, the Germans cut through Poland at great speed. To make matters worse for the Poles, in mid-September the Russians invaded Poland from the east. Polish resistance collapsed and Germany and Russia divided Poland along the 'Ribbentrop-Molotov Line'. A Polish government in exile was set up in London to try and continue the struggle but effectively Poland - and the prospect of an eastern front - had disappeared. The Germans were now able to transfer the bulk of their army to the west.

France and Britain had done little to help Poland. The French, aware of the terrible casualty lists of the First World War, had no intention of launching a serious offensive against German frontier fortifications, even though only about a third of the German army was in the west in September 1939. Years would elapse before Britain was in a position to send large numbers of well-equipped troops to the Continent. Chamberlain had no wish for a shooting war and remained confident that economic blockade would bring Germany to its knees.

In October Hitler offered vague but possibly genuine peace proposals to Britain and France. There were certainly good reasons for the Western democracies to make peace. War against Germany was likely to be terribly expensive in terms of blood and treasure. The only countries likely to benefit were those that remained neutral. But few British politicians were prepared to trust Hitler and sacrifice Poland.

There was thus no peace and for several months not much war to speak of either. This was the period of 'Phoney War'. All the opposing armies were content to await behind their respective defensive lines. No country wished to be the first to launch massive aerial assaults on cities. In Britain more people died from road accidents caused by black-out restrictions than from bombing. Only at sea was there a reminder that this was a real war. Fortunately Germany did not yet have sufficient U-boats to pose a severe challenge to Allied shipping routes. Neither Italy nor Japan tried to exploit the situation at this stage so the worst fears of British defence planners remained in abeyance.

The main country to exploit the situation was Russia. In October the Baltic States - Estonia, Latvia and Lithuania - were forced to accept Soviet garrisons. Stalin then turned on Finland but the Finns resisted his demands for territory. In November 1939 Russia invaded Finland. To everyone's surprise, the Finns fought with skill and bravery and held up the vastly superior Russian forces. Many politicians, (especially Churchill), thought Britain and France should send help to Finland and fight the USSR as well as Germany! An elaborate plan to send 100,000 troops to Finland, via Norway and Sweden, enabling the Allies to cut off Swedish iron ore supplies to Germany, was finally devised. 'The only charitable conclusion is to assume that the British and French governments had taken leave of their senses', wrote A.J.P.Taylor. Certainly Allied planners massively miscalculated the potential strength of the USSR. But in March 1940, just as the Allied force was about to move, the Russo-Finnish war came to an abrupt end. Finland ceded territory to Russia but not as much as Stalin had initially demanded.

Although the allies could no longer help Finland, the idea of blocking Swedish ore to Germany was not abandoned. The winter supply route went via Narvik in Norway and then down the Norwegian coast to Germany. In April 1940 the Allies decided to block this route by laying mines in Norwegian territorial waters. The day after the allies began mining, Germany occupied Denmark and the main towns in Norway. The Danes simply surrendered. Norway tried to resist and accepted the offer of Allied help. But the British and French Norwegian campaign was badly planned and executed and by the end of April Allied forces were evacuated from most of Norway.

On 7-8 May 1940 the Norwegian campaign was debated in the House of Commons. Many MPs were angry at the way the campaign had been conducted. Strangely their target was not Churchill, who had been largely responsible for the operation, but Chamberlain. Criticism of the Prime Minister had been mounting; many felt that he failed to project vigour and vision. His statement, just a few days before the Norwegian campaign, that Hitler 'had missed the bus', wrankled. During an intense debate, Leo Amery, a leading Conservative backbench MP, in a wide-ranging attack, finished by pointing at Chamberlain and quoting the words of Oliver Cromwell to the Rump Parliament: 'You have sat too long for any good you have been doing. Depart, I say, and let us have done with you. In the name of God go!'

About 40 Conservative MPs voted against the Government and a further 60 abstained. The Government had a majority of 81 but this was far less than their usual majority of over 200. Chamberlain was clearly losing the confidence of the House and probably the nation as well. Discussions took place as to how the Government might be strengthened. Labour leaders said they were prepared to serve in a coalition Government but not under Chamberlain. Chamberlain decided he must resign. There were really only two possible successors -

Lord Halifax (the Foreign Secretary) or Winston Churchill. Churchill was the most popular member of the Cabinet, epitomising Britain's will to victory. However he was not as popular in the Cabinet or in Parliament. His record over the previous three decades had often been suspect and Chamberlain, King George VI and many Conservative MPs would have preferred Halifax. Halifax, however, realising it would be difficult to run the war from the House of Lords, was not eager to become Prime Minister. Churchill had no such inhibitions! He was convinced he was the right man for the job and on 10 May he became the new Prime Minister.

Churchill formed a new government which included not only Chamberlain and Halifax but also Labour and Liberal leaders. Party differences were transcended in the common struggle but Churchill made it clear he intended to be the supreme director of the war on the military side. In a speech to the Commons on 10 May Churchill admitted:

1 I have nothing to offer but blood, toil, tears and sweat. . . .You ask, What is our policy? I will say: it is to wage war, by sea, land and air, with all our might and with all the strength that God can give us: to wage war against a monstrous tyranny, never surpassed in the dark, 5 lamentable catalogue of human crime. That is our policy. You ask, what is our aim? I can answer in one word: Victory - victory at all costs, victory in spite of all terror, victory, however long and hard the road may be; for without victory there is no survival.

2 Britain Alone

The first weeks of Churchill's new Government coincided with a series of military disasters. On 10 May 1940 German forces invaded Holland and Belgium. Other German units broke through the French line near Sedan and drove a great wedge between the Allied armies in France. Within ten days German tanks had reached the English Channel. Most British troops were deployed to the north of the German thrust and evacuation seemed the only alternative to annihilation. At the end of May and the start of June, around 350,000 British and Allied troops were evacuated from Dunkirk in a motley collection of vessels. Dunkirk is sometimes viewed as a success. Certainly the number of men who managed to return to Britain far exceeded the most optimistic forecasts at the start of the operation. But as Churchill admitted, 'Wars are not won by evacuations.' The evacuated troops were forced to leave behind all their heavy weapons and transport and returned to Britain in a chaotic and demoralised state.

France's position was now desperate. On 10 June Italy joined the war on Germany's side. Although French forces fought well against the Italians, elsewhere the Germans continued their advance. Churchill made several visits to France to try to encourage the French government to resist but had little to offer except words. The French government, after anguished debate, decided to surrender and on 22 June accepted the German armistice terms. North-west France was put under German military occupation. The remainder kept its own government, now sited at Vichy. General Charles de Gaulle escaped to Britain but his 'Free French' organisation had few supporters at this stage. The debate about who was most responsible for the fall of France goes on. The British tend to blame French politicians and military leaders. Many French, on the other hand, still argue that Britain had not exerted herself to the full and should have fought at rather than fled from Dunkirk. This debate was academic in the summer of 1940. What mattered was that Britain was now alone against a Nazi-dominated Europe. For some, from King George VI downwards, the release from Continental entanglements was almost a bonus. At least there would be no immediate Western front slaughter. Nor was Britain quite alone. She had the support of the Empire, which could provide vital raw materials and large numbers of troops. Even so Britain's position seemed hopeless. Nobody, not even the optimistic Churchill, could look forward to the day when British forces might land again on the Continent and defeat the Germans. Nor was there any reasonable prospect of bombing or blockading Germany into surrender. Instead there was a real possibility that German forces would now overrun Britain.

In July 1940 Hitler launched another 'Peace Offensive'. He was prepared to guarantee the British Empire in return for Britain accepting German conquests in Europe. He was confident that Britain would agree to his relatively lenient terms. It is possible that either Chamberlain or Halifax might well have accepted the terms. But a defiant Churchill resolved, and exhorted the British people, to fight on. He made it plain that his government would never 'parley' with Hitler.

There is little doubt that Churchill reflected the views of the vast majority of Britons who were determined to continue the war and, somehow, against all military logic, bring it to a successful conclusion. Most British people believed that Hitler could not be trusted and so there was little prospect of a long-lasting peace. No-one wanted to believe the war was lost. Churchill, confidently citing history and pointing out that Britain had held out before in similar circumstances, helped convince his fellow-countrymen that the war could be won.

At the end of July Hitler gave orders for a massed air offensive against Britain, to be followed by a cross-Channel assault in September, 'if we have the impression that the English are smashed'. The Germans, however, had not anticipated having to move against Britain so quickly and were not really ready. Hitler, already contemplating a war against Russia, never seems to have had much conviction in 'Operation Sealion'. But if the Luftwaffe had destroyed Britain's air power, a German invasion would probably have been improvised. The Battle of

Britain, therefore, was vital to Britain's survival.

That battle had no formal start or end but most British historians agree that it lasted from mid July to mid September 1940. At the outset the Luftwaffe had some 4,550 planes compared to the RAF's 3,000 - of which only about 800 were Hurricane or Spitfire fighters. In early September the RAF was perilously close to defeat. But the Germans blundered by turning away from bombing radar stations and air-bases to bombing London. This gave the RAF time to recover and on 15 September, 'Eagle Day', they destroyed over 50 German aircraft (not the 183 claimed at the time). By simply remaining as a viable force, the RAF effectively won the Battle of Britain. Any plans Hitler might have had to invade Britain were postponed.

The Germans now turned their attention to night bombardment of cities, especially London. Although some 45,000 people died in the 'blitz', the Germans did not possess enough bombers to have any chance of shattering the British economy or civilian morale. All they succeeded in doing was generating a durable anger among most Britons.

In November 1940 Chamberlain died and Halifax soon went as Ambassador to Washington. Anthony Eden now became Foreign Secretary, a post he was to retain until July 1945. The main task of Churchill, Eden and all British diplomats in 1940-1 was to find allies. Churchill remained optimistic, convinced that the logic of events would eventually cause the USA and the USSR to become engaged on Britain's side; and that this 'Grand Alliance' would prove irresistible.

From the start President Roosevelt had sympathised with the British cause. In 1939 he and Churchill had begun a private correspondence which became a vital channel for Anglo-American relations throughout the war. In late 1939 Roosevelt had persuaded Congress to allow the Allies to purchase arms on a 'cash and carry' basis. After the fall of France, Roosevelt was even more prepared to give Britain assistance. America now provided Britain with 50 clapped-out destroyers in return for the right to establish bases in British possessions in the West Indies. Roosevelt talked about the USA becoming the 'arsenal of democracy' and in March 1941 signed the Lend Lease Bill which made enormous quantities of American resources available to Britain. Opinion polls in the USA consistently revealed massive sympathy for the British cause. However, although the USA was hardly strictly neutral, most Americans still had no wish to actually get involved in the war.

The USSR gave Britain no sympathy at all. Sir Stafford Cripps, the left-wing lawyer sent as ambassador to Moscow to try to improve Anglo-Russian relations, was kept at arms length by Stalin. Britain had nothing to offer the USSR in adequate compensation for a break with Germany. Cripps wrote gloomily in August 1940 that if the Russians had to choose between the two sides 'there is no doubt whatever they would choose Germany'. However, German-Soviet relations did give Britain some hope. Russia's annexation of the Baltic States and ambitions in the Balkans angered Hitler. The 1939 Nazi-Soviet Pact was simply a marriage of convenience. Hitler loathed communism and dreamed of winning living space (lebensraum) in the east. Nevertheless, Germany seemed to be doing rather better at winning allies than Britain in 1940-1. In September 1940 Germany, Italy and Japan drew up the Tripartite Pact. Fortunately this was a rather vague expression of friendship rather than a fully-fledged alliance and Japan did not yet join the war. Mussolini was Hitler's chief ally in 1940-1. Italian forces threatened Britain's position in Egypt and the Middle East. Churchill believed that control of the Suez Canal was essential, so much so that he was even prepared to send troops to Egypt when Britain herself faced the threat of invasion. An Italian invasion of Egypt in September 1940 was soon defeated and Britain followed this up by occupying Italian Somaliland, Ethiopia and much of Libya (see the map on page 22). An Italian invasion of Greece in October 1940 also failed.

These Italian disasters were a blow to Axis prestige. There was also the possibility that the French in North Africa might go over to Britain and that Britain might establish a permanent foothold in Greece. The Germans, therefore, sent General Rommel and the Afrika Korps to Libya to bolster the Italians. They also put increasing pressure on Greece to submit to humiliating terms. The Greeks determined to resist. In March 1941 there was a coup d'etat in Yugoslavia. The new government was anti-German. In April 1941 the Germans attacked and quickly overran both Yugoslavia and Greece, driving out an ill-fated British expeditionary force as they did so. They went on, after a spectacular parachute attack, to capture Crete. Meanwhile, General Rommel inflicted a series of defeats on the British forces in North Africa.

The only way Britain could strike at Germany was bombing. But British bombing raids had little pattern, purpose or success. Casualties among air crews were almost as great as German civilian casualties! German U-boats were far more effective than British bombers. Germany had rapidly increased her U-boat fleet and by 1941 was winning the Battle of the Atlantic. Although Churchill talked optimistically about being given the tools and then being left to finish the job, without allies it seemed inconceivable that Britain could ever defeat Hitler.

3 The Grand Alliance

On 22 June 1941 Hitler launched 'Operation Barbarossa' - the invasion of Russia. This caused greater surprise in Russia than it did in Britain. British intelligence knew of the impending attack several weeks before it occurred but efforts to alert Stalin to the danger had failed. Churchill said privately that, 'If Hitler invaded Hell, I would at least make a favourable reference to the Devil in the House of Commons'. He now declared that, 'the cause of any Russian fighting for his hearth and home is the cause of free men and free people in every quarter of the globe . . . we shall give whatever help we can to Russia.' Within weeks Britain and Russia concluded an agreement for mutual assistance.

Many British experts anticipated an early Russian collapse as German forces advanced eastwards. But although the Red Army suffered heavy casualties, it continued to fight, and as Churchill observed, what mattered was not so much where the Russian front happened to lie, but that the front was still in existence. From Britain's point of view the good news was that she now had an ally who was able to absorb the greatest weight of the German military machine.

In July 1941 Stalin asked Britain to launch an attack in the west to divert German forces from Russia. Churchill would like to have helped and pressed for an attack in Norway or Normandy. But the British Chiefs of Staff finally convinced him that even a small-scale diversionary attack was out of the question. The only way in which Britain could effectively help Russia was in the matter of supply. Unfortunately there was no easy way of sending material to Russia and there was the added problem that Britain herself was short of military supplies. President Roosevelt, however, agreed to extend Lend-lease to Russia.

In August 1941 Roosevelt and Churchill met off Placentia Bay in Newfoundland and agreed to a joint statement of principles - the 'Atlantic Charter'. This committed America to the desire for a 'final destruction of the Nazi tyranny'. The Charter also made it clear that the Allies were fighting for a wide range of 'freedoms', not for any territorial goals. The vagueness of some of the phraseology helped to conceal the latent differences between America and Britain on certain matters. The Charter was useful for Roosevelt who still needed to assure domestic opinion that the British-Russian cause was worth supporting. Churchill reported to the War Cabinet that Roosevelt had said he would wage war but not declare it. Roosevelt was certainly edging the USA nearer to war. Already in July 1941 US forces had occupied Iceland. The USA also undertook responsibility for the escort of all convoys from America to the mid-Atlantic. This inevitably brought US ships into conflict with German U-boats. But it was events in the Pacific, not the Atlantic, which finally brought America into the war.

From 1939 Britain had relied on the USA to deter Japan from exploiting the situation in the Far East. American-Japanese relations had deteriorated steadily throughout 1940-1. In 1941, rather than attack the USSR, Japan turned her attention southwards, taking over French Indo-China. Britain and America retorted by freezing all Japanese assets. The USA went further and imposed an oil embargo on Japan. Japan had now to decide whether to withdraw from China and Indo-China (as the USA demanded) or seize more territory in the south from which it could get the raw materials (especially oil) it needed to go on fighting. Such an expansionist policy was bound to lead to war with the USA and Britain. In October a new government took office in Japan determined to bring matters to a head. Intense diplomatic efforts continued through November but Japan and the USA failed to reach agreement.

On 7 December 1941 the Japanese attacked Pearl Harbor and destroyed a large part of the American Pacific Fleet. Immediately afterwards Japan declared war on Britain and the USA. Both Britain and the USA had expected a Japanese attack but they did not know precisely where or when, and neither had made effective preparations. From Britain's point of view this hardly mattered. The important thing was that the USA was now in the war. Churchill later said, 'he went to bed and slept the sleep of the saved and thankful.'

On 11 December Germany and Italy, honouring the commitments of the Tripartite Pact, declared war on the USA. This, according to A.J.P.Taylor, was an act of 'gratuitous loyalty or folly'. If Hitler had not declared war, America might well have concentrated its energies on the war against Japan rather than on the war in Europe.

Churchill rushed across the Atlantic to meet Roosevelt. Both leaders confirmed that over-all priority should be given to a 'Europe first' strategy, which had been tentatively agreed upon in secret pre-war planning. General strategy and operational control were to be co-ordinated through a Combined Chiefs of Staff. Roosevelt invented a grand name - the United Nations - for the various Allied powers, and in January 1942 all joined in a declaration that they would wage war together and not make a separate peace. Churchill's visit was a great personal success and he returned from Washington well pleased.

While Churchill was in America, Eden visited Moscow. This visit was not so friendly. Stalin seemed more concerned with Russia's post-war position than with the war itself. He proposed a secret treaty whereby Britain would accept Russia's acquisitions of 1939-40 and in return Russia would support aspirations which Britain might have for bases in Western Europe. Eden was in no position to sign such a document, even if he had wished to do so. It would contravene not merely Britain's guarantee to Poland but also the Atlantic Charter. It was clear that Stalin had little time for the idealistic vision of the Atlantic Charter and was determined to maintain Russia's 1941 frontiers.

Churchill's immediate reaction to Stalin's border proposal was sharp. The Baltic States, he declared 'were acquired by acts of aggression in shameful collusion with Hitler'. The transfer of their peoples against their will would be 'contrary to all the principles for which we are fighting this war and would dishonour our cause'. There was considerable debate on the matter both in Britain and America. Finally in May 1942 Britain and Russia signed a long-term alliance which made no mention of frontiers. However, Eden did concede that Britain acknowledged Russia's position in the Baltic States.

In May 1942 Molotov, the Soviet Foreign Minister, pressed the Allies to launch a direct attack on German-occupied Europe. US leaders favoured the idea but the British were far more cautious. Military chiefs pointed out that the Allies lacked sufficient men, aircraft and landing craft. In August Churchill visited Moscow to explain there could be no Second Front in 1942. Although Stalin looked 'very glum' at this news, he seemed to have been impressed by Churchill's talk of strategic bombing and the proposed Allied landings in North Africa. For all their suspicion, the two men established a working relationship and parted amicably.

The 'Grand Alliance' between Britain, the USA and the USSR meant there was now every likelihood of ultimate victory, although in what form, so far as Britain's world power was concerned, was unpredictable. Churchill already mistrusted Stalin and, for all their common ties, the USA and Britain had different approaches to world affairs. As the USA harnessed her vast resources for war, it was clear that Britain would be the poor relation. The fact that Roosevelt regarded the British Empire with suspicion, an obstacle to American commerce and an affront to the concept of self determination, was a cause for concern.

In 1941-2, however, the main problems for Britain were military rather than diplomatic. In the Far East Britain and America suffered appalling defeats at the hands of the Japanese. The loss of Singapore in February 1942 was described by Churchill as 'the worst disaster . . . in British History'. By the summer of 1942 Japanese forces were threatening Australia and India. German forces continued to be successful in North Africa and Russia. The Battle of the Atlantic went badly. By 1942 the Germans had nearly 400 U-Boats and every month merchant shipping losses rose.

4 The Turn of the Tide

During 1942-3 the Allied military situation improved. In the summer of 1942 Japanese expansion was checked decisively in the battles of the Coral Sea and Midway. The Battle of the Atlantic also turned dramatically in favour of the Allies. By the summer of 1943 Atlantic shipping losses were substantially reduced and a large number of U-boats were sunk. The Atlantic became a relatively safe seaway. This meant that the huge American build-up of men and supplies in Britain proceeded largely unhindered. In 1943 Allied air raids finally began to inflict damage on German cities. The US airforce adopted a policy of daylight raids aimed at particular targets. Britain continued to attack German cities by night. Just how much damage was inflicted is debatable. The German economy, which was only now fully gearing itself for war, was not devastated by the bombing but attacks on some industrial targets, such as oil refineries did take their toll.

In November 1942 General Montgomery defeated Rommel at the battle of El Alamein in Egypt. This gave Churchill the fillip of a major - British - victory. Rommel was forced to retreat across Libya and Axis hopes of capturing the Suez Canal ended. An Anglo-American force, under the command of the American General Eisenhower, landed in French Morocco to add further pressure. Vichy French resistance to the invasion quickly crumbled. For a while the Allies' main problems were political rather than military. They had to decide which French leader to deal with. There were several possibilities. But increasingly it became obvious that the difficult and arrogant General de Gaulle could not be ignored, much as Roosevelt would like to have ignored him.

The real turning point came in Russia. By autumn 1942 German

Europe and North Africa 1939 – 45

forces had reached Stalingrad. Fierce fighting took place over the winter. Finally in January 1943 the German troops surrendered. Stalingrad, often seen as the decisive battle of the Second World War, was followed by other Soviet victories, notably the battle of Kursk, and German forces in Russia began a slow retreat.

The Russians, doing most of the hard fighting and tying down most of the German forces, continued to press the Allies to open up a Second Front. Most Americans supported an immediate attack on France, believing the Allies should not waste time and effort on subsidiary theatres of war. In Britain there was a massive campaign for a Second Front, especially from the Left. Churchill, convinced that the idea of a seaborne attack on France was militarily unsound, resisted the pressure. In 1942-3 Churchill still played a dominant role in determining Allied strategy. Although US strength was growing rapidly, British forces in Europe still outnumbered the Americans, and weight of numbers tended to determine weight of influence. Churchill continued to favour military action in the Mediterranean, not so much because he thought this would benefit the British Empire (as many Americans suspected) but more because he thought it would help to win the war. Given that so many Allied troops were already in North Africa, the logical next step was an attack on Sicily followed by a campaign in Italy. This offered the opportunity of attacking the Axis on the 'cheap' without the likelihood of enormous manpower losses which Churchill felt might occur if there was an early confrontation with German forces in France.

In January 1943 Roosevelt and Churchill met at Casablanca in Morocco and Churchill persuaded the reluctant President to agree to an Allied invasion of Sicily. The two leaders also discussed future war aims and agreed that the Axis powers must unconditionally surrender. This decision has been criticised by some historians, who argue that it resulted in the Germans and Japanese people fighting desperately to the bitter end even when the war was clearly lost. It certainly gave Axis propaganda a useful weapon. However, 'unconditional surrender' probably made little difference. The German and Japanese leaders and many of their people were determined to fight to the end and the Allies were already committed to total victory.

In July 1943 the Allies, now in total control of North Africa, invaded and quickly occupied Sicily. This led to the overthrow of Mussolini. The new Italian government began secret negotiations for an armistice. It now made sense, even to those American military chiefs who supported an immediate invasion of France, to invade the Italian mainland. A meeting between Churchill and Roosevelt at Quebec in August confirmed that the US would indeed support an Italian campaign, provided Britain gave priority to invade France in 1944. The Allied invasion of Italy began in September 1943 and the Italian government immediately announced that it had changed sides. This made little difference. The Germans rushed forces into Italy, restored Mussolini, but henceforward treated the country as occupied territory. The Allied advance up the Italian peninsula developed into a long slogging match. Aneurin Bevan's description of the Allies 'climbing up the backbone', seemed more appropriate than Churchill's idea of the 'soft underbelly'. But the Allies did force the Germans to divert resources from the Eastern front, and did push northwards, entering Rome in June 1944.

Meanwhile the Russians advanced westwards. This meant that it became increasingly difficult to postpone decisions on the future of Poland. In 1943 the USSR proposed that the eastern frontier of Poland should follow roughly the 'Curzon Line'. This Line, drawn up by the Allies in 1919 as a potential but never an actual frontier, was similar to the dividing line between German and Soviet occupation of Poland in September 1939. Poland would be compensated for her losses in the east by gaining territory at Germany's expense in the west. The Polish government in exile in London had no intention of giving away any territory and its relations with the USSR rapidly deteriorated. The discovery, by the Germans, of a mass-grave of 8-10,000 Polish officers in Katyn forest made matters worse. These officers, the Germans (correctly) declared, had been murdered by the Soviet authorities in 1940. The Russians declared (wrongly) that the Germans themselves were responsible for the atrocity. The Polish government in exile proposed that the International Red Cross should investigate the matter. The USSR responded by breaking diplomatic relations with the London Poles. Churchill faced something of a dilemma. He thought that the German revelations were 'probably true' but realised that Hitler hoped to use the Katyn discovery to drive a wedge between the Western Allies and the USSR. He, therefore, largely ignored the Katyn massacre.

Despite continuing arguments over Poland, relations between the Russians and the Western Allies remained generally good. All the 'Big Three' seemed determined to leave aside political differences in order to win the war. Roosevelt, despite his special relationship with Churchill, did not intend to let himself be put in a position where Britain and the USA automatically united against Russia. He hoped that Stalin, suitably handled, would work for a world of peace and democracy. The Teheran Conference in November 1943, the first attended by Roosevelt, Churchill and Stalin, was in many ways the high water mark of Allied unity. For Churchill, however, Teheran was something of a disaster. Roosevelt showed he was prepared to isolate Churchill and deal directly with Stalin and it was clear that British influence was fading. Churchill later remarked:

> There I sat with the great Russian bear on one side of me, with paws outstretched, and on the other side the great American buffalo, and between the two sat the poor little English donkey who was the only one . . . who knew the right way home.

The main outcome of the Teheran Conference was that Churchill and Roosevelt agreed to invade France in May 1944 while Stalin agreed to attack Japan after the end of the German war. There was also some discussion of Poland's future. Churchill was prepared to accept Stalin's frontier proposals for Poland but his efforts to bully the London Poles into acceptance met with little success. Meanwhile the military build-up in Britain in preparation for 'Operation Overlord' - the invasion of France - continued. By 1944 there were some 500,000 US servicemen in Britain. The Germans knew that an attack on 'Fortress Europe' was coming. What they did not know was when and where. General Eisenhower, the Allied Supreme Commander, did all he could to keep them guessing.

5 Victory

On 6 June 1944 - D Day - Anglo-American forces landed on the Normandy beaches in France and established a permanent bridgehead. It took weeks of hard fighting before the Allies were able to force their way inland. But in mid-August German resistance, first in Normandy and then throughout France, collapsed. Paris was liberated and Allied troops advanced into Belgium and Holland. By 1944-5 Allied aircraft enjoyed almost complete control of the air. German cities were now bombed unmercifully. Bombing raids on Dresden in February 1945 killed at least 30,000 (and possibly nearer 100,000) people.

The Russians continued their inexorable advance in the east. The major problem as far as Britain was concerned was who would control various parts of Eastern Europe after the war. Poland remained a particular area of concern. The Polish government in exile was still unwilling to work with either the Russians or the Russian-backed Polish 'Committee of National Liberation', soon based at Lublin. Events in Warsaw in August and September 1944 aggravated the situation. Expecting Russian assistance, people in the Polish capital rose up against the occupying Germans. But the Russians gave no help and the rising was brutally crushed.

Churchill was increasingly worried about Russian aims and apparent American aimlessness with regard to Eastern Europe. An Anglo-American Conference at Quebec in September 1944 achieved little. 1944 was a Presidential election year and Roosevelt refused to be drawn on questions of relations with the USSR until after the election. In October 1944 Churchill and Eden went to Moscow. Churchill and Stalin failed to reach agreement over Poland but had more success in discussing the rest of Eastern Europe. Churchill later described what happened:

1 The moment was apt for business, so I said, 'Let us settle our affairs in the Balkans. Your armies are in Rumania and Bulgaria.

We have interests, missions and agents there. Don't let us get at
cross-purposes in small ways. So far as Britain and Russia are
5 concerned, how would it do for us to have 90% of the say in
Greece, and go for 50-50 about Yugoslavia?' While this was being
translated I wrote out on a half-sheet of paper:
>   Rumania
>   Russia 90%
10   The others 10%
>   Greece
>   Great Britain
>   (in accord with the United States) 90%
>   Russia 10%
15   Yugoslavia 50% - 50%
>   Hungary 50%- 50%
>   Bulgaria
>   Russia 75%
>   The others 25%
20 I pushed this across to Stalin, who had by then heard the
translation. There was a slight pause. Then he took his blue pencil
and made a large tick upon it and passed it back to us. It was all
settled in no more time than it takes to set down.

Although it was difficult to say precisely what 10 per cent Allied and 90
per cent Russian influence in Rumania might mean in practice,
Churchill was delighted with this agreement. On his return to Britain, he
declared that, 'Our relations with the Soviet Union were never more
close, intimate and cordial than they are at the present time'. Stalin's
good faith was soon demonstrated in action. Attempts by communists to
seize power in Greece were thwarted by British troops. Stalin made no
effort to help the Greek communists and a pro-British monarchical
government was set up. But Churchill still feared the ambitions of the
Soviet leader. This fear intensified Churchill's desire to see a resurrected
France which might stand with Britain against the USSR. This would be
essential given the real possibility that American troops might withdraw
from Europe at the end of the war.

In November 1944 Roosevelt was re-elected and realised the need for
a top-level Conference to resolve urgent problems. In February 1945,
Churchill, Roosevelt and Stalin met at Yalta in the Crimea. Agreement
on several matters, such as the principle of the future occupation of
Germany and its division into three occupation zones, had been reached
before the Yalta meeting. But the Big Three were able to resolve a
number of issues. Churchill won reluctant acceptance from the other
two for the proposal that a military zone for France should be carved out
of the area proposed for Britain. There was agreement that there should
be free elections in the countries of liberated Europe. Stalin agreed to
join both the United Nations and the war against Japan within three

months of the war against Germany ending. Agreement was also reached on Poland's frontiers. The eastern frontier was fixed on the lines which Stalin had proposed long before. Poland's western frontier was to be the Oder-Neisse river line which meant that a good deal of Germany would come under Polish rule. After long negotiations a form of words was accepted as to the character of the interim Polish government before 'free and unfettered' elections were held.

Since 1945 there have been many criticisms of the Yalta agreements. Some historians have argued that a frail and dying Roosevelt was misled into making too many concessions to Russia. After the war Churchill expressed similar views, claiming he had wanted to take a tougher line on a number of issues at Yalta and had received no support from Roosevelt. However, it is hard to see how Britain or the USA could have taken up a different position at Yalta or got better terms. Soviet forces already effectively controlled much of Eastern Europe. Roosevelt's main concerns were to end the fighting against Germany and Japan as quickly as possible, and to remain on good terms with Stalin after the war. At least Stalin had committed himself to the United Nations (Roosevelt's great hope for the future) and to war against Japan. The Yalta Conference ended in a blaze of apparent friendship and Churchill returned to London saying he had 'every confidence in Stalin'.

But Churchill was soon shaken by reports from Poland. The Polish communists seemed more concerned with arresting and executing enemies than with civil liberties. In March 1945 Churchill wrote to Roosevelt urging him to take a tougher line on the USSR and expressing fears that they 'had underwritten a fraudulent prospectus' at Yalta. In late March Eden wrote in his diary, 'I take the gloomiest view of Russian behaviour everywhere . . . our foreign policy seems a sad wreck'.

The military situation caused less anxiety. In March 1945 Allied forces finally crossed the Rhine and cut deep into Germany. Churchill wished to press on and capture Berlin ahead of the Russians but Eisenhower refused. By this stage in the war, the US was increasingly calling the tune. By 1944 US armament production was six times as great as Britain's and the Americans had more men in Europe than Britain. Eisenhower had no wish to suffer more casualties than was necessary. Plans for dividing Germany into occupied zones had already been worked out and captured territory in East Germany would have to be handed over to the USSR.

Roosevelt's death in April 1945 came as a shock to Churchill. The new American President, Harry Truman, was an inexperienced and unknown quantity, and it would take time to establish the close relationship which Churchill had built up with Roosevelt. The deaths of Mussolini and Hitler at the end of April came as less of a shock. On 8 May Germany finally surrendered. The European conflict was over. The war against Japan, however, had still to be won.

Churchill was in no mood for rejoicing. He wrote that at the moment of victory 'apprehension for the future and many perplexities . . . filled my mind as I moved about among the cheering crowds'. A few days later he wrote to Truman warning him of Russia's powerful military presence in Europe and used the term 'Iron Curtain' to describe the barrier which existed between the region of Europe occupied by the Russians and that occupied by the Western Allies. He was anxious that American forces should remain in Europe. The US administration, however, was not so convinced that Stalin was a threat to future world peace. Churchill was also at odds with British opinion. Many Britons, aware of Russia's valiant resistance, regarded Stalin as a kindly 'Uncle Joe' and, thanks to Labour propaganda, viewed the USSR as a kind of workers' paradise.

In Britain the Labour Party decided that the moment had come to withdraw from the wartime coalition. A general election was called for July. The Conservatives hoped that Churchill's prestige and popularity would be enough. But he fought a lack-lustre campaign and did not convince the public that he or the Conservatives had a clear idea of what they wanted to do with the future. The Labour Party concentrated on the crucial themes of housing, social insurance and full employment. Voting took place on 5 July but problems involved in collecting votes from the forces overseas delayed the declaration of poll for three weeks. This meant that both Churchill and Attlee, the Labour leader, attended the start of the Potsdam Conference in July 1945. The thinking was that if Attlee were to become Prime Minister he could easily pick up the threads of policy. In the event Labour won a massive majority and Attlee it was who formed a new government.

The change of government in Britain had little effect on the Potsdam Conference which was mainly concerned with issues arising from the occupation of Germany. Some progress was made here but there was deadlock over almost every other subject. During the Conference President Truman told Stalin that the Americans, after years of research, had developed a new weapon, the atomic bomb, which he hoped would shorten the war against Japan.

It had seemed likely that Japan might continue fighting for many more months. Although the Allies were pushing the Japanese back, they continued to meet ferocious resistance. Truman, fearing the Allies might sustain more casualties than in the war against Germany, determined, with the approval of both Churchill and Attlee, to use the atomic bomb. On 6 August the new bomb was dropped on Hiroshima, killing tens of thousands of people. Although there has been much criticism of the dropping of the bomb since, a decision not to drop the bomb would have been hard to make and even harder to justify in August 1945. Two days later Russia declared war on Japan. The next day a second atom bomb was dropped on Nagasaki. The Japanese government at last agreed to surrender.

6 Winston Churchill

Winston Churchill has long been regarded as one of Britain's greatest Prime Ministers. Recently, however, revisionist historians, such as John Charmley, have questioned Churchill's 'greatness'. Certainly the Churchill of myth (and his war memoirs!) was not always the Churchill of history. However most historians are still convinced that Churchill was an inspired and inspiring war leader, 'the saviour of his country'.

a) Background and Character

Churchill's whole life seemed to have been dedicated to preparing him for leadership in the Second World War. He had held most of the important government offices and was a formidable negotiator and first-rate administrator. He knew more about war than any other 20th-century British Prime Minister. He had tremendous confidence in himself. In his memoirs Churchill recalled his emotions on becoming Prime Minister: 'I was conscious of a profound sense of relief. At last I had the authority to give direction over the whole scene. I felt as if I were walking with destiny.' Most of those who knew Churchill, and most historians who have studied him, stress his prodigious energy, his incredibly active mind, and his moral and physical courage. However, there were character defects. He was totally self-centred. He quickly became irritable and depressed. He was erratic. Many feared his lack of judgement. He was rarely able to resist an unconventional idea, sometimes to Britain's benefit, sometimes not.

b) His Leadership 'Style'

From the start Churchill struck a consistent pose of courage and resolve. Eccentric in dress, speech and gesture, he caught and kept the confidence of the public. Many have stressed the importance of his oratory. Churchill, himself, made a more modest assessment: 'It was the nation and the race dwelling all round the globe that had the lion's heart. I had the luck to be called on to give the roar'. The 'Dunkirk spirit' of 1940 was certainly not something that was conjured up by Churchill. Most British people in 1940 were determined to fight to the end, whoever had been Prime Minister. Nevertheless the 'roar' was important. Churchill's speeches in the Commons and his radio broadcasts (often heard by over 50 per cent of the country) nearly always succeeded in hitting the right note. In the darkest days of the war, his declarations that Britain would never surrender helped sustain morale.

But Churchill was much more than a voice. He was Chairman of the War Cabinet and Minister of Defence. He determined military strategy. He settled disputed questions in domestic matters. He conducted in person most of the important negotiations with Britain's international partners. He dominated his staff. Most people were in awe of his eloquent tongue and it was not easy to stand against him.

Churchill could not and did not do everything. His influence over his colleagues in the War Cabinet was powerful but not paramount. There were instances of his being overruled. His influence was sometimes restricted by his frequent absences, through illness or journeys abroad. He had little interest in domestic matters and tended to leave these to Labour politicians. However the buck ended with Churchill, and he was quite happy to take the responsibility. Indeed he was in his element. A.J.P.Taylor said, 'He never drew breath. In this turmoil of activity he made some great mistakes and many small ones. The wonder is that he did not make more. No other man could have done what he did, and with a zest which rarely flagged'.

c) Churchill and Military Strategy

Churchill was the supreme director of the British war effort. He appointed and dismissed generals, admirals and air marshals. The orders to them were issued in his name. He considered himself an expert on war. (He had been a serving army officer, had directed the Admiralty in two World Wars and written books about war.) Consequently he interfered with military operations more than any previous Prime Minister had ever done.

Churchill was criticised at the time, and has been criticised since, for his strategic conduct of the war: for his over-estimation of what could be achieved by naval and air power; and for his under-estimation of the difficulties in the way of the fulfilment of his plans. He has been criticised for a host of military disasters - Norway in 1940; Greece, Crete, Singapore in 1941-2. Some historians continue to claim that the Allies should have launched a Second Front in France in 1943 rather than in 1944. Churchill is also charged with supporting the indiscriminate bombing of Germany which is viewed by many as being both immoral and ineffectual. Many have criticised him for interfering too much and particularly for replacing capable commanders, such as Dowding, who led the RAF to victory in 1940 yet was dismissed soon afterwards.

It is also possible to over-rate Churchill's successes. These were sometimes due to the fact that Britain was able to intercept and decipher many of the high-level Axis radio messages. Britain's code-breakers at Bletchley Park (often known as Ultra) provided increasingly good information as the war progressed. The fact that Ultra was kept secret until 1973 gave the impression for many years that some of Churchill's decisions were more inspired than was really the case.

However, Churchill has his defenders. His readiness to interfere with almost any aspect of the war may have been a constant trial to his subordinates, but his constant probings, suggestions and demands at least imparted a sense of urgency to all who came under his scrutiny. He usually supported the policy of his military 'professionals', rarely overruling the advice he was given. The disasters which did occur were the outcome of decisions which the Chiefs of Staff had approved. To his credit Churchill did forge a military team that won success. 'Before El Alamein we never had a victory. After El Alamein we never had a defeat', boasted Churchill, with some justification. It should also be said in Churchill's favour that Britain avoided the slaughter of the First World War. His reluctance to launch a Second Front in 1943 can certainly be supported. Neither Britain nor the USA was prepared for a seaborne assault on France and failure would have been costly in lives and could have set back the war effort by several years. Even the strategic bombing of Germany can be defended. It was one of the few ways that Britain could actually make war on Germany and the raids did have damaging effects on German war production.

Some historians think that if Churchill had been in the 'driving seat' in 1944-5, the Allies would have captured Berlin, much of East Germany and the Balkans ahead of the Russians. What Churchill described as the 'Iron Curtain' would then have been much farther east. However, in 1944-5 Churchill did not actually press very hard for some of the anti-Russian policies which he and others later claimed he supported. His main concern was to defeat the existing enemies rather than prepare to deal with hypothetical future worries.

d) Churchill the Diplomat

Churchill did not conduct foreign policy in 'splendid isolation'. Although he provided the broad lines of policy, it was Foreign Secretary Eden who followed these up. The two men worked reasonably well together, even if Churchill's methods of work were sometimes as trying to Eden as they were to the Chiefs of Staff.

Churchill saw it as his main task to weld the 'Grand Alliance' together and to ensure that the strategy pursued was the best to accomplish the downfall of the enemy. In seeing himself as the lynchpin of the Alliance, he possibly exaggerated his influence. Stalin and Roosevelt were certainly prepared to go their own ways, and even to join together on occasions against him. He tended to rely too much upon his personal relationships with the Russian and American leaders, confident that things would somehow work out. However, many historians praise Churchill for his statesmanship and for his hard work in keeping an unnatural alliance - British imperialism, American capitalism and Soviet communism - together. Although the eldest of the 'Big Three', he was certainly the most peripatetic, meeting Stalin five times and Roosevelt ten times, often travelling by air at a time when such journeys were dangerous and uncomfortable.

The fact that he had an American mother gave him a head start in forming close ties with America. He helped convince Americans and their President to assist Britain in the dark days of 1940-1. Once the USA had entered the war, he established cordial relations with Roosevelt and with other leading US political and military figures. But relations were not always easy. American policy was geared, in part, to promoting British decolonisation and there were endless tensions over China, Persia, India, Palestine and Egypt. By 1944 America increasingly dominated the Anglo-Saxon alliance and did not always act in ways which Churchill perceived to be in Britain's best interests. Churchill was particularly critical of the USA's policies with regard to the USSR.

Britain's relations with the USSR have been criticised for being both too hard and too soft - and (with more justification) for being inconsistent and impulsive. Relations with the USSR were always likely to be difficult, given the ideological gulf separating the two leaders. However, Churchill recognised that it was essential to work with Russia and, by tact and forbearance, succeeded in building up a working relationship with Stalin. The main problem, for historians now and Churchill then, was understanding Stalin's aims. Was he motivated by fear or ambition? Churchill, for the most part, assumed Stalin was driven by ambition and his responses to Russian policy were based on this assumption. Some historians think that opportunities were missed to win the confidence of Stalin by honest and generous diplomacy. They see Churchill's suspicion of Stalin as being an important contributory factor in the causes of the Cold War. However, other historians are of the view that the Western leaders - especially Roosevelt - failed to take a strong stand against Stalin's wartime demands, especially on Poland, thereby encouraging him to become even more exacting.

Churchill's claim that if the USA had only listened to him, the Western powers would not have conceded control of Eastern Europe to the USSR is an important one (and an important pit-prop for Churchill's reputation!). However, recent historians have criticised this view pointing out that Churchill's policy to Russia fluctuated widely and that America by 1945 was ready to stand firm against Russian infringements of the 'spirit of Yalta'.

e) Churchill's Legacy

By fighting and winning the Second World War, Britain destroyed Hitler and Nazism and ensured that Germany did not dominate Europe. But, in many respects the war was hardly a glorious success for Britain. She failed to save Poland and failed to keep (Russian) totalitarianism out of Europe. The war, moreover, weakened Britain's international position. By 1945 she was outclassed by the USA and the USSR. It is thus possible to claim that Britain's finest hour was her gravest error. To what extent was Churchill to blame for this situation?

Churchill can certainly be blamed for his part in propelling Britain

Main Military Events		Main Political/Diplomatic Events
September: Germany overran Poland November: Russia attacked Finland	**1939**	September: Start of the war
↑ Phoney War ↓	**1940**	
April: Germany overran Norway and Denmark May-June: Germany overran Belgium, Holland and France July-September: Battle of Britain		May: Churchill made Prime Minister September: Tripartite Pact
The Blitz	**1941**	March: Lend Lease
April: Germany overran Yugoslavia and Greece June: Germany attacked USSR		August: Churchill met F.D.R: Atlantic Charter
Dec: Pearl Harbor. USA entered war		Dec./Jan: Churchill visited USA
February: Fall of Singapore	**1942**	August: Churchill met Stalin
Oct./Nov: Battle of El Alamein November: Allies invade Morocco		
Jan: Germans surrendered at Stalingrad May: Germans surrendered in N. Africa	**1943**	January: Casablanca Conference August: First Quebec Conference
September: Allies invade Italy		November: Teheran Conference
June: Operation Overlord Allies invade France August: Paris liberated Russians push into Germany	**1944**	
		Sept: Second Quebec Conference October: Churchill met Stalin
	1945	February: Yalta Conference
March: Allies cross Rhine and invade Germany from West		April: Deaths of Roosevelt, Mussolini and Hitler May: Germany surrendered July: Gen. Election - Labour victory July-August: Potsdam Conference
August: Hiroshima and Nagasaki		August: Japan surrendered

Summary - The Second World War

into war in 1939. Arguably Chamberlain's government had a much steadier grasp of realities of British power in the late 1930s than the impulsive Churchill. Some historians (eg Charmley) have gone further, however, and criticised Churchill's war-leadership. The major charge levied against him is that he concentrated solely on defeating Hitler and failed to consider Britain's role in the post-war world. Consequently, in order to stop Hitler, Churchill bankrupted Britain, mortgaged her future to the USA, and helped raise the Russian spectre in Europe - a menace even greater than the one destroyed. How could this have been averted? Charmley argues that it may have been in Britain's best interests to have made peace with Hitler in 1940-1. British power, Charmley claims, might then have been left intact while the communists and the Nazis slugged it out in Eastern Europe to the eventual benefit of Britain.

These views are worth serious consideration. However, they can never be more than 'ifs'. In reality, for better or for worse, Britain had gone to war with Germany in 1939. Once involved in conflict, there was little alternative but to fight to the bitter end. A negotiated peace with Hitler was out of the question as far as most Britons were concerned. Hitler could not be trusted and therefore had to be defeated. The only way to defeat him was to ally with the USA and the USSR. By 1945 both these countries were far more powerful than Britain. But at least Britain had emerged victorious from the Second World War. If Britain was henceforward to be a US satellite, this was far better than being a German protectorate. Churchill's reputation as a great war leader, although under attack, has not yet been seriously damaged. It is still easier to argue that he was the right man in the right job at the right time.

Making notes on 'The Second World War'

You need to make fairly full notes on this chapter. The headings and sub-headings in the text should help you to organise your note-making. It is worth making a conscious effort to distinguish between 'facts' and 'interpretations' in your notes. You do need to know a solid core of facts to support your arguments. With interpretations, the most important thing is to grasp the essential ideas rather than the details. Try writing down a very brief summary (normally no more than one sentence) of the interpretation in your own words. Then try adding extra details. Your notes should help you to assess Britain's role in the Second World War and especially the skill and achievements of Winston Churchill. You will have to make up your own mind about Churchill and the options open to him. Might he have been better advised trying to reach a negotiated peace with Germany, especially in 1940-1? Was it really in Britain's best interests to ally with the USSR and the USA? How grand was the 'Grand Alliance' and was Churchill the lynchpin of the alliance? Should Churchill be blamed for Britain's situation in 1945?

Answering Essay questions on 'The Second World War'

It is likely you will use evidence from this chapter to answer specific questions about the conduct of British foreign policy in 1939-45. Consider the following questions:
1   Why was the British government unwilling to reach a negotiated peace with Nazi Germany after September 1939?
2   Assess critically the achievements of Winston Churchill in foreign affairs from 1940 to 1945.

The golden rule for writing history essays is simple: answer the question set and not the one you wish had been set! The first paragraph - or introduction - is often crucial. It is the first opportunity for you to impress (or depress) an examiner. There is no perfect way of writing an introduction but there are certain things you ought to be trying to do. Firstly you should be trying to establish the precise meaning of the question. This often involves defining the most important terms in the title and also identifying the periods of time which are relevant. You should also be identifying the key issues within the question which you will go on to develop. Finally you should also outline your basic argument. It is a waste of time and space to say (as many students do) that you are going to answer the question. Hopefully you are so get on and do it from the start!

Try to write an introduction for Question 1. Try and compose a good opening sentence. Go on to identify the periods of time which are relevant. You clearly need to cover the whole period from September 1939 to May 1945. But there were certain times when a negotiated peace was more likely than others. Remember that most of the peace initiatives came from Hitler. Why did Britain not respond? Why was the British government unwilling to make peace with Germany before May 1940? Why was Churchill unwilling to make peace in 1940-1? Why did Churchill support 'unconditional surrender' after 1942-3?

Another essential part of the essay is the final paragraph or conclusion. In this you should be recapping, drawing together the threads of your argument and finally giving your opinion on the central issue in the question set. Your conclusion should not be loaded down with factual information. Nor should you spring some new and previously unexplored idea that you have just thought of on the reader. The conclusion should stem logically from the rest of the essay. Do not be afraid to give your view: after all, this is what questions usually ask for. But try not to use phrases like, 'I think' or 'in my opinion'. A personal view does not sound very authoritative. It is far better style to write 'the evidence suggests' or 'it seems likely that'.

Try writing a conclusion of six to eight sentences for Question 2. The question asks you to be critical. This means you should try to be both positive and negative. What were Churchill's main diplomatic successes? What were his main failures? Did his successes outweigh his failures - or vice-versa? Did he really have much control over events? Did he achieve his aims? Try and reach a balanced conclusion but note that this doesn't mean you should sit on the fence. At the end of the day are you going to praise or blame Churchill - and why?

Source-based questions on 'The Second World War'

1 Churchill May 1940: 'blood, toil, tears and sweat'.
Read carefully the extract from Churchill's speech to the House of Commons on May 10 1940, given on page 13. Answer the following questions:
a) How had Britain been 'waging war' prior to May 1940? (4 marks)
b) Why might historians i) praise and ii) criticise the tone of Churchill's speech? (6 marks)
c) How might Churchill have envisaged victory being achieved in May 1940? (5 marks)
d) What do you think was the purpose behind Churchill's speech? (5 marks)

2 Churchill's view of the Teheran Conference
Read carefully Churchill's view of the Teheran Conference, given on page 22. Answer the following questions:
a) Explain Churchill's comment: 'the great Russian bear on one side of me, with paws outstretched'. (3 marks)
b) Explain the phrases: 'the great American buffalo' and 'the poor little English donkey'. (3 marks)
c) Why might Roosevelt and Stalin have not been keen to follow Churchill's 'right way home'? (4 marks)
d) Churchill's account was written several years after the Teheran Conference. Does this effect the value that this source might have for historians? (5 marks)

3 Changes in Eastern Europe 1944
Read the extract in which Churchill describes doing business with Stalin in October 1944, given on pages 23-4. Answer the following questions:
a) Why was Churchill so keen for Britain to be involved in the Balkans? (4 marks)
b) Why was Churchill so pleased with the agreement? Did he have good cause to be pleased? (6 marks)
c) Why might Roosevelt have been critical of this Anglo-Soviet agreement? Explain your answer. (5 marks)
d) What does this extract indicate about the way in which Churchill conducted diplomatic business? (5 marks)

CHAPTER 3

Post-war Problems, 1945-8

1 The Situation in 1945

Britain emerged from the Second World War victorious and apparently relatively unscathed. Although she had lost about 400,000 people, this was only about half the number she had lost in the First World War and only about one fiftieth the number of Russian dead. The scale of destruction in British cities bore no comparison with much of Europe, especially Germany. She had escaped the rigours of enemy occupation and the British economy seemed far ahead of the war-shattered economies of Europe. Moreover, Britain had come out of the war with her massive Empire intact. Victory in 1945, as in 1918, seemed a striking vindication of the Empire's strength and solidarity.

In 1945 Britain was certain to be one of the main arbiters of the post-war peace settlement. She was still acknowledged as one of the Big Three - equal to the USA and the USSR. Her forces had played a major part in the Allied victory. Those forces (which in 1945 numbered 5,000,000 men) were stationed all over the globe - in Germany, Austria, Italy, Greece, Palestine, Persia, Iraq, Syria, North Africa, Indo-China and the Dutch East Indies, as well as in many parts of the Empire.

However in 1945, although Britain sat at the same diplomatic tables, she could not compare in size and strength with the USA and the USSR. The USSR had done most of the hard fighting against Germany and, despite the catastrophic devastation of its territory, possessed in 1945 a tremendous array of conventional forces. The USA emerged from the war as easily the richest country on earth. Subject neither to bombing or invasion, the US economy had thrived under the stimulus of war. By 1945 the USA produced about 50 per cent of the world's manufactured goods. She was also a great military power. As well as possessing large, well-equipped conventional forces, she was the only country with the ability to manufacture atomic bombs.

Britain's main problem was the fact that she lacked the economic resources to match the two great superpowers. The Second World War had exacerbated Britain's long-term economic problems. The physical destruction of houses, factories and shipping had cost the country about 25 per cent of its national wealth. Most foreign assets had been sold to pay for essential war-time imports, thus significantly reducing the income from abroad that had previously contributed to Britain's economic strength. As a result of the war British industry had failed to modernise and re-equip. In 1945 British exports totalled £350 million - 40 per cent of the pre-war figure - while imports had reached £2000 million. This massive trade deficit would not be easy to remedy. Valuable markets had been lost, mainly to American competitors and it was likely to take Britain many years to restructure her industries for peacetime production. Britain was also in debt to the tune of over £3,500 million. Repayment of this debt seemed impossible. Indeed in 1945 there seemed the real possibility that Britain would simply run out of hard currency and be unable to import the supplies of food, fuel and raw materials on which her economy depended. American assistance was vital. But many British officials were already troubled by the extent of Britain's dependence upon the USA, wondering how far dependence on American loans was compatible with Britain's existence as an independent great power.

Economic weakness meant that Britain needed to reduce both her overseas commitments and her armed strength. But, given the unstable world situation, this would not be easy. In 1945 there were profound fears in Britain about the aims of the USSR. The Russians already controlled most of Eastern Europe, and Greece, Turkey, Iraq, Iran and even Italy, seemed vulnerable to Soviet pressure. It seemed likely, therefore, that Britain would need to maintain a massive military presence in Europe in order to deter any Soviet threat. Safeguarding her many global bases was also likely to impose a great burden on Britain's defence budget and trouble was already looming in India and Palestine.

There were other problems. Europe was in chaos. There was a vast refugee problem, little political stability, and economic devastation. And, as in 1919, the future of Germany remained a major problem. At least the future of Germany and other central and East European countries would largely be determined by the various wartime arrangements which had defined areas of military occupation. The fate of Eastern Asia, by contrast, had not been resolved by wartime agreements. Britain, America, Russia, the Nationalist Chinese of Chiang Kai-shek, the Communist Chinese of Mao Tse-tung, the French, and the Dutch all had - often conflicting - claims to make in terms of influence or territory.

2 The Labour Government

The Labour government, which triumphed in the July 1945 general election, had to face these problems. Never before had a Labour government had an overall majority in the House of Commons and many pundits predicted that there would be a major shift in British foreign and imperial policy. Certainly there were some important differences between Labour and Conservative policies. The Labour Party had a long-standing aversion to 'imperialism' and 'militarism'. The new government was committed to granting independence to India and also committed to promoting self-government, where possible, within the Empire. Moreover, Labour had always been less pro-American and more sympathetic to the USSR than the Conservative Party and some Labour MPs in 1945 talked of developing a distinctly 'socialist' foreign policy. Sir Orme Sargent, soon to become Permanent Under-Secretary in the Foreign Office, feared a 'Communist avalanche over Europe, a weak foreign policy, a private revolution at home and the reduction of England to a second-class power'.

Clement Attlee, the 62-year-old Labour Prime Minister, was in many ways an establishment figure - a public school-Oxbridge product, who represented intellectual rather than working-class socialism. Churchill's description of him as a 'sheep in sheep's clothing' was unfair. (He had been Deputy Prime Minister since 1943 and had chaired the War Cabinet!). Although not a dominating personality, he was a tenacious politician and an excellent team leader. He led an experienced Cabinet team, many of whose members had served in Churchill's National Government.

Attlee delegated considerable responsibility in external affairs to Ernest Bevin, the self-made, former Transport and General Workers' Union leader who was his surprise - some thought inspired - choice as Foreign Secretary. Bevin's qualification for the job seemed slight. Although he was an experienced and skilful administrator, his main interest before 1945 had been in labour relations and economic affairs - he had been Minister of Labour in Churchill's Inner War Cabinet. However, he had a special interest in foreign affairs throughout the war and had established good relations with both Churchill and Eden. The working-class Bevin (who continued to drop his 'h's) made no sweeping changes in the public school personnel of the Foreign Office and indeed quickly became devoted to the career diplomats. They in turn grew to respect Bevin who proved himself (not surprisingly given his trade union background) a shrewd and tough negotiator, bringing (many thought) a robust and practical common sense to diplomatic affairs. Having decided on his policy, he had the personal authority to carry it in Cabinet, invariably with the full support of Attlee.

The view that Attlee and Bevin would steer British foreign policy in a sharply leftwards direction was to prove false. Both men were determined to preserve Britain's world-power status and to defend Britain's interests against all comers. Neither wished to be seen as the liquidators of the British Empire. Bevin, in particular, was determined to preserve the entirety of British power. Nothing would be given up, unless circumstances forced him to. Both Attlee and Bevin believed that Britain's economic difficulties would prove temporary and that Britain's industrial base and international trading system, based on the Empire, would soon recover. Both men had a deep detestation of communism, born of their long struggles to exclude it from the Labour Party and the union movement. Bevin, like Churchill, believed that Britain must stand up to Russia (he prided himself on knowing how to handle communists!) and thought that co-operation with the USA was the best way to prevent the expansion of Russian power.

3 The Problem of the USSR

In 1945 the hope, perhaps even the expectation, was that the wartime coalition of Britain, the USA and the USSR would continue. There was also faith in the United Nations as a mechanism for regulating international affairs. However, there were profound fears in some quarters in Britain (more so than in the USA) about the immediate aims of the USSR. Many, like Churchill, believed that Stalin could not be trusted and feared he intended to stir up world-wide communist revolution.

Russian sympathisers (then and since) have argued that Stalin, far from threatening to disturb the status quo, feared attack by capitalist countries. All he wanted (it is claimed) was a protective zone of sympathetic states on Russia's borders. He certainly seems to have pursued a remarkably passive policy in Greece and to have had little influence over the Chinese communist Mao Tse-tung. At first sight the fears which Churchill expressed about Russian threats to Europe (and Asia) might seem exaggerated. In 1945 Britain and America had a combined population in excess of the USSR. Their technology was in most respects superior and their productivity far greater. The USA also had the atom bomb. The USSR, therefore, was not in a position to use its superiority in conventional forces to coerce the West.

However, most Western historians now believe British (and later American) policy-makers were right to suspect Stalin, whose record, at best, seems to have been one of extreme ruthlessness balanced by cautious opportunism. Russian secrecy and the fact that neither he nor Molotov, the Russian Foreign Minister, would say precisely what it was they wanted was also a persistent barrier to understanding. Not surprisingly Attlee and Bevin came to the conclusion that Russia was motivated more by ambition than by fear - and responded accordingly. Bevin soon considered both Stalin and Molotov to be 'evil men' and believed that the USSR was fundamentally hostile to all that the British and American societies stood for.

Although there was no immediate break with the USSR, Anglo-Soviet relations steadily deteriorated in 1945-6. This became evident in a number of conferences that were held between the Foreign Ministers of the four Allies (the Big Three, plus France) in an effort to agree on peace terms with their former enemies. There were serious problems with Germany. Potsdam succeeded in settling the final boundaries of the zones of occupation, including the special arrangements for Berlin which was to be jointly occupied by the four Powers. In theory Germany was to be treated as a single unit, both economically and politically, but as each occupying power began to extract reparations from its own zone this meant that the economic division of Germany began from the first days of the Allied military occupation. There was no agreement on a long-term solution simply because neither the West nor the USSR could afford to risk a united (and still potentially powerful) Germany siding with the other.

There was also alarm in Britain about the situation in Eastern Europe where it was clear that the USSR was not honouring the British understanding of the Yalta agreements. Communist domination of Poland, Bulgaria, Hungary and Rumania, although not total, was fast becoming a reality. Only in Czechoslovakia did a precarious balance exist in government between Russian-supported communists and politicians in the western tradition. Greece remained Britain's only foothold in the Balkans. Even here it seemed possible that the pro-British Greek government might be overthrown by communist insurgents. There was also alarm in Britain about Russian ambitions in both the Mediterranean (where the Russians put increasing pressure on Turkey) and in the Middle East (where the Russians were slow to withdraw troops from northern Iran).

The Soviet threat was highlighted by Winston Churchill. In a famous speech at Fulton, Missouri, in March 1946 he declared:

1 From Stettin in the Baltic to Trieste in the Adriatic, an iron curtain has descended across the Continent. Behind the line lie all the capitals of the ancient states of Central and Eastern Europe. Warsaw, Berlin, Prague, Vienna, Budapest, Belgrade, Bucharest
5 and Sofia. All these famous cities and the populations around them lie in the Soviet sphere and all are subject, in one form or another, not only to Soviet influence but to a very high and increasing measure of control from Moscow. Athens alone . . . is free to decide its future . . .
10   However, in a great number of countries, far from the Russian frontiers and throughout the world, Communist fifth columns are established and work in complete unity and absolute obedience to the directions they receive from the Communist centre . . .
    On the other hand, I repulse the idea that a new war is
15 inevitable, still more that it is imminent. It is because I am so sure that our fortunes are in our own hands and that we hold the power to save the future, that I feel the duty to speak out now   . . . I do not believe that Soviet Russia desires war. What they desire is the fruits of war and the indefinite expansion of their power and
20 doctrines . . . From what I have seen of our Russian friends and allies during the war, I am convinced that there is nothing they admire so much as strength, and there is nothing for which they have less respect than for military weakness.

Churchill's intention was to shake the Americans into an awareness of the Russian threat. He spoke only as leader of the opposition. But many people in the USSR and the USA saw his Fulton speech as a major statement. The speech went down badly in some quarters in Britain

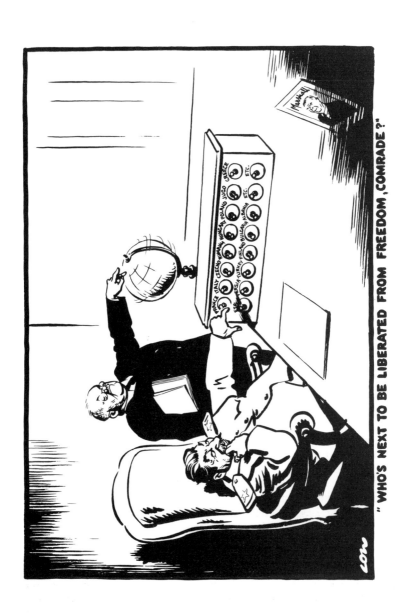

'Who's next to be liberated from freedom, Comrade?', David Low cartoon

where hope for co-operation with Stalin still lingered. However, neither Bevin nor Attlee voiced any disagreement with Churchill's comments. Like Churchill, they drew on the 'lessons of appeasement' and agreed that it was better to stand firm than to give in to a potential aggressor. Bevin and Attlee's suspicion of Russia did not mean that they wholly despaired of achieving tolerable relations with Stalin. Attlee remained more optimistic than Bevin of reaching some agreement within the United Nations framework. Both Prime Minister and Foreign Secretary believed there was a need for a mixture of firmness and understanding. Nevertheless by the end of 1946 it was clear that every move to extend Russian influence whether in Eastern Europe, the Mediterranean or the Middle East would be opposed by Britain, preferably in concert with the USA.

4 Relations with the USA, 1945-6

Some British politicians, such as Churchill, saw co-operation with the USA as essential for Britain's security and economic recovery. However, others were deeply troubled by the extent of Britain's dependence upon the USA and feared that Britain was in danger of becoming simply an American satellite. Some on the left were suspicious of America as the citadel of capitalism. Others on the right saw the USA as a dangerous rival, determined to better its economic interests at Britain's expense.

Attlee and Bevin, aware of the need for US support in Europe, were anxious that the close relationship established with America during the war should continue. Unfortunately many Americans did not share the British government's enthusiasm for close collaboration. Most Americans had no wish to prop up the British Empire and there was considerable mistrust of the socialist experiment being undertaken by the Labour government.

Bevin's main fear was that the 'erratic' Americans would repeat their post-1918 pattern and retreat into isolation, leaving Britain to face the USSR alone. In 1945-6 such fears seemed well-founded. US troops in Europe were run down from 3.5 million in June 1945 to 200,000 in 1947. Isolationist voices in the USA remained strong. Within America there was also an influential China lobby which argued that the Far East was far more important to the USA than Europe. Many Americans, wary of getting dragged into what they saw as old-style Anglo-Russian power politics in Europe, dismissed Britain's fears of Russian aims. For much of 1945-6 the American administration still hoped for co-operation with the USSR.

Behind the scenes British and American military leaders, anxious about Soviet policy, maintained informal contacts under cover of the continued existence of the wartime Combined Chiefs of Staff. But Britain needed US official help and this was not immediately forthcoming. The lack of US support was particularly worrying in two areas - finance and the atomic bomb.

In August 1945, following the surrender of Japan, the USA suddenly announced the end of Lend-Lease. Hugh Dalton, the Chancellor of the Exchequer, said Britain faced 'total economic ruin' if more American financial aid was not forthcoming. A strong team of British negotiators, headed by the distinguished economist Lord Keynes, was sent to Washington. Keynes was confident of securing an $8 billion grant, interest free, on the grounds of Britain's wartime sacrifices. Such hopes proved utopian. Many Americans thought of Britain, not as a junior partner, who had impoverished herself in a just war, but as a powerful, potential trading rival who should be forced to dismantle her Empire and imperial preference. However, hard bargaining eventually produced an American offer to write off Britain's Lend-Lease debts (worth some $21 billion) for $650 million, and to provide a loan of $3.75 billion at 2 per cent interest. In return, Britain was forced to agree (in principle) to dismantle her system of imperial preference and to promise that all holders of sterling should be able to convert their pounds into dollars in 1947.

Compared with the situation after 1918, and given the state of American public opinion, these were very generous terms. But many British MPs bitterly resented them. Two ministers, generally regarded as spokesmen of the 'left', Aneurin Bevan and Emanuel Shinwell, fought strenuously against acceptance of the terms in Cabinet fearing that Britain would be left at America's mercy in world trade. However, the majority of the Cabinet believed that Britain had no option but to accept the terms. Without an American loan the domestic reform programme would suffer and Britain would have no alternative but to cut military commitments overseas. Despite Labour and Conservative opposition, the loan agreement was pushed through Parliament in December 1945.

The atomic bomb had been developed during the war as an Anglo-American project. Preliminary British research had been invaluable. But as the project advanced the USA had rapidly become the dominant partner. In 1943 Churchill had secured from Roosevelt agreements that required British approval before the bomb could be used. In November 1945 Truman pledged 'full and effective co-operation in the field of atomic energy' between the USA, Britain and Canada. But during 1946, under pressure from a spy-scared Congress, he went back on his word and in August 1946 approved the Macmahon Act which forbad the exchange of atomic information with any country, including Britain.

5 British Defence and Financial Problems

Given the USA's determination to retain her nuclear monopoly, Attlee thought Britain had no alternative but to develop her own atomic research programme. Hugh Dalton and Stafford Cripps opposed the idea on financial grounds but the Chiefs of Staff were in favour as was Bevin who at a crucial meeting of senior Cabinet members in October 1946 argued that 'we've got to have this thing over here whatever it costs ... We've got to have the bloody Union Jack flying on top of it'. Work on the British nuclear bomb started in earnest in January 1947. The decision was concealed from all but the senior members of the Cabinet and from Parliament for the next 5 years. Attlee had no doubts about the rightness of the decision:

1 If we had decided not to have it, we would have put ourselves entirely in the hands of the Americans. That would have been a risk a British Government should not take . . . There was no NATO then. For a power of our size and with our responsibilities to turn
5 its back on the Bomb did not make sense.

Faced with an apparent Soviet threat, Attlee's government also decided to maintain strong conventional defences. Substantial British forces were kept in Germany, demobilisation proceeded slowly and conscription was maintained - an unprecedented step in peacetime. By 1946-7 there was growing disaffection within the Labour Party over Britain's defence spending and conscription. Hugh Dalton insisted that in order to balance the books overseas military commitments must be reduced and industrial exports quickly increased. These two issues were closely linked because more men in the armed forces meant less for industry.

The worst financial drain was Germany. International failure to agree on a peace settlement meant that the occupation troops remained and that the German economy was kept near to subsistence level, with basic needs supplied by the occupying power in each zone. Britain controlled North-West Germany, the most industrialised and heavily war-damaged area. In 1946 Britain provided 70 per cent of her occupation zone's food at a time when bread rationing had been imposed in Britain. Such a situation could not continue indefinitely. In July 1946 Britain and the USA agreed to fuse their zones, regardless of Russian objections, and to start increasing German industrial production to encourage self-sufficiency. But the 'bizone' which came into existence in January 1947 did not immediately solve the financial situation and it only worsened relations with Moscow.

In 1946 Attlee, who anticipated no real danger of war with Russia until 1950 at the earliest, proposed defence cuts in the East Mediterranean. He told the Cabinet's Defence Committee that it 'was not necessary in present circumstances to have a large fleet ready for instant action as there was no one to fight' and argued that British forces in the region might actually provoke rather than deter. The threat of a mass resignation by his Chiefs of Staff, however, persuaded Attlee not to make immediate cuts to British commitments in the East Mediterranean.

However, the bitter winter of early 1947 forced the government's hand. Freezing cold and heavy blizzards brought transport, industry and the coal mines to a virtual halt for several weeks. Manufacturing output fell sharply and the balance of payments deficit widened alarmingly. Dalton warned the Cabinet that Britain was racing through the US dollar credit at a 'reckless, and ever-accelerating, speed' and predicted 'a looming shadow of catastrophe'. By February 1947 Attlee's government was desperate to find ways of reducing its external commitments.

6 The Truman Doctrine and Marshall Aid

Since 1944 British troops had been stationed in Greece to support the government against communist insurgents. The troops remained after 1945 as Greece moved closer to civil war. The cost of British assistance was considerable - £132 million in 1945-6. By the end of January 1947, Attlee's government decided that it could no longer afford to aid Greece. However, it seemed certain that Greece would fall under communist control if British troops withdrew. The USSR would then be in a strong position to exert pressure on Turkey and to control the East Mediterranean. The only possible way to stop communist domination was if the USA assumed responsibility for defending Greece (and Turkey) against communism. Bevin and the Foreign Office had been working hard for months to persuade the USA to accept responsibility.

Behind the problem of Greece was the much greater question of whether the USA would take over from Britain the prime responsibility for the defence of Europe. Many prominent Americans opposed such a policy on the grounds that such involvement would entail risks and costs out of proportion to the possible benefits. Nevertheless by early 1947 many US diplomats and politicians had come round to the belief that there was a serious Soviet threat and that it must be opposed.

Informed in February 1947 of Britain's intention to pull out of Greece, Truman's response was rapid and momentous. His new Secretary of State George Marshall, an implacable opponent of the USSR, prompted Truman to take up the British burden. In March Truman appealed to Congress for $250 million for Greece and $150 million for Turkey. But his appeal went beyond these two countries. The President portrayed the proposed aid programme in apocalyptic terms as part of a global struggle between democracy and totalitarianism. It must, he argued, be the policy of the USA 'to support free peoples who are resisting attempted subjugation by armed minorities or by outside pressure'and sought not just money but authority to send American forces if necessary, to help threatened peoples. This was the so-called Truman Doctrine. The President's appeal was successful and Congress voted $400 million for aid to Greece and Turkey. The Truman Doctrine indicated that American foreign policy had changed: from now on the USA would offer concrete support to help contain the

Russian threat. The implications for Britain were immense and reassuring.

In late April 1947 Secretary of State Marshall returned to America from a visit to Europe convinced that Europe was likely to disintegrate politically, socially and economically - to the benefit of the communists - unless America offered immediate economic assistance. In June 1947 Marshall made a celebrated speech at Harvard University in which he offered Europe economic aid. His main aims were to restore stability and prosperity to Europe, thus saving Europe from communism, and

THE TRUMAN LINE

Punch *cartoon, 28 May 1947*

thereby safeguarding the security and prosperity of the USA. Marshall, emphasising that Europe must assume responsibility for its own economic recovery, invited the European nations to meet to detail their needs and promised that America would respond to them. The so-called 'Marshall Plan' was not so much Marshall's at all but more ... invitation to others to devise their own plans.

Bevin greeted Marshall's proposals as a 'lifeline to a sinking man'. By the summer of 1947 the 1945 American loan was almost exhausted, Britain had a serious balance of payments deficit, and there was a disastrous run on Britain's gold and dollar reserves. Although Bevin would have preferred Britain to have received special treatment, he devoted all his energies to co-ordinating the full European response for which Marshall had called. In late June the Foreign Ministers of Britain, France and the USSR met in Paris to discuss the Marshall Plan. Marshall had said that he regarded Russia as a European nation and Bevin hoped that the Russians might 'play after all'. However, Stalin (as Marshall had anticipated) had no intention of co-operating with the West. Denouncing the American proposals as 'dollar imperialism', a blatant American device for gaining control of Europe, he forbade the East European governments from participating in the plan.

Britain and France were determined to proceed. In July they invited all European states (except Spain) to join in framing a reply to Marshall's proposals. A 16 nation Committee of Economic Co-operation was established. Before the end of September this Committee presented Marshall with a 4 year plan for European economic reconstruction. The plan was duly accepted and the 16 (West European) nations established the permanent Organisation for European Economic Co-operation (OEEC) in April 1948. Between 1948 and 1951 the USA provided about $12 billion for the OEEC to administer. Britain received the largest share - $2.6 billion. Marshall Aid accomplished nearly all its aims. European production dramatically increased and a prosperous Western Europe showed little inclination to go communist.

The unfortunate side effect of Marshall's offer and the Soviet rejection of it was to sharpen the division of Europe into two economic groups, one looking to the USA, the other to the USSR for leadership. By the summer of 1947 the vestiges of co-operation between the communist and non-communist forces in Europe had largely disappeared. A Foreign Ministers' Conference which met in December 1947 ended in mutual recriminations with no further meetings planned. The gloves were off between Russia and the West. They remained so in virtually every quarter of the globe for the next four decades.

7 The Empire/Commonwealth in 1945

In 1942 the British Empire in Asia had seemed on the verge of destruction. Malaya, Singapore, Burma and Hong Kong had been lost and even India and Australia seemed to be in jeopardy. However, Britain's fortunes had been remarkably transformed by the summer of 1945. Japan's surrender in August enabled British forces in South-east Asia to regain former territories and it could be proudly claimed that no British colonies had been permanently lost as a direct result of foreign conquests. One quarter of the world's land surface, therefore, remained part of the British Empire or Commonwealth, as it was now commonly called. The Empire/Commonwealth had been vital to Britain's war effort. Throughout the war the dominions and Britain's colonies had provided manpower and vital raw materials. Some thought the war had strengthened the Empire/Commonwealth by promoting a sense of common purpose.

In other respects, however, the war had served to weaken imperial ties. It had emphasised the difference of interest between Britain and each of the 'white' dominions. Ireland had not even fought on Britain's side in the war and many South Africans had not wished to fight. By 1945 Australia, Canada and New Zealand had all slipped into America's orbit. In 1940 Canada had set up a Joint Defence Board with the USA, the first alliance contracted between a dominion and a foreign power. Even before 1941, Australia had been uneasy about the effectiveness of Britain's Far East defences. With the fall of Singapore and the subsequent collapse of British power in South East Asia, the inability of Britain to defend Australia and New Zealand was obvious. With Australia threatened by Japanese invasion, the Australian Prime Minister declared openly, 'Australia looks to America, free of any pangs as to our traditional links with the United Kingdom'. By 1945 the old sense of strategic dependence on Britain had vanished and co-operation between Britain and the dominions could no longer be taken for granted.

The war had seen Britain mobilise the Empire's resources to an unprecedented degree. Colonial economies were regulated by government controls over output, prices, marketing and labour. Opposition to British rule in India and Egypt had been forcibly suppressed. Regimentation and suppression led to increased opposition to British rule in some colonies.

The war had undermined the foundations of British imperial power in other ways. Japanese success shattered British prestige in Asia - prestige on which colonial rule so heavily depended. Even though Britain, with American backing, had ultimately triumphed against Japan, the Japanese wartime victories are usually seen as a real stimulus to Asian independence.

The war had also created new international conditions, both politically and economically. The ideological struggle against Hitler had made assertions of pre-war colonial principles unfashionable. Although many British politicians (probably) still believed that the white race was superior, it was less easy to openly claim it. Moreover, the two great superpowers, the USA and the USSR, were ideologically anti-colonial in outlook and their opposition to empire was likely to influence the hopes of colonial peoples. Before 1939 Britain's economic strength had helped bind all the countries of the Empire/Commonwealth to the British imperial system. But Britain's weakened economy in 1945 boded ill for empire. If Britain was too poor to buy what the dominions and colonies produced, too poor to invest in their economic development, and unable to provide the manufactured goods they needed, one of the most significant factors holding the Empire together would be lost.

Although some left-wing Labour MPs were anxious to see an end to the Empire, this was not the opinion of Attlee's Cabinet. Most ministers realised that without her colonies (and their rich resources), Britain would no longer be a great power and her economic prosperity would be threatened. Only in India was the Labour government committed to granting independence.

8 India, 1945-8

The future of India was perhaps the most difficult problem facing Attlee in 1945. Throughout the inter-war period many educated Indians had pressed for independence from Britain. The main vehicle for Indian home rule demands had been the Congress Party, whose leaders included Gandhi and Nehru. British governments pre-1939 had made several important concessions and it seemed only a matter of time before India was granted dominion status. However, in September 1939, the British Viceroy, on his own authority and without consulting a single Indian, had pledged the support of India to the British cause - a serious rebuff to those Indians who wanted home rule.

Indian leaders were divided on how to respond to the war. Gandhi, a pacifist, opposed any support for the British war effort. Some Indian nationalists, believing Britain's plight was India's opportunity, were prepared to work with Germany and Japan. The Congress party as a whole refused support for the war effort unless India could participate as an independent state. However, Mohammed Ali Jinnah, leader of the Muslim League, strongly supported the war, hoping he might thus win British support for a separate Muslim state of Pakistan.

In 1942, as the Japanese army advanced towards India's borders, there was serious disorder within India. A divided British Cabinet finally agreed to offer India full independence after the war in return for political support during it. Congress leaders, settling for nothing short of immediate full independence, turned down the British offer. A great non-co-operation movement - 'Quit India' - followed. British authorities took firm action. Over 1,000 Indians were killed and nearly 100,000 were arrested. By November 1942 the authorities had the situation under control. Significantly, the Indian army remained loyal to Britain.

For three years Congress was out of effective action. Jinnah was thus well placed to extend the influence of the Muslim League in those northern provinces where the Muslims were a majority.

In 1945 Churchill, believing it was possible to pursue a policy of divide and rule, was convinced that Britain could and must hold on to India - vital not only for its size but also for its role as provider of the army of empire. But Attlee's government, and particularly Attlee himself, was committed to granting Indian independence. The mounting costs of the Raj reinforced the Labour government in its view that the time had come for Britain to leave India, and to leave quickly before what remained of British power was overwhelmed by (possibly violent) events. There was also a fear of adverse international (especially American) opinion if Britain tried to cling to power.

Attlee hoped that an independent India would remain united and within the Commonwealth, looking to Britain for guidance and leadership out of free choice, not out of compulsion. In this way Britain might actually benefit from Indian independence. She would no longer have the burden of having to keep large numbers of troops in India and yet might (hopefully) be able to rely on the Indian army to safeguard her interests in Asia. But both these aims - Indian unity and ensuring that India remained within the Commonwealth - were likely to be difficult to achieve. Worsening relations between (the Hindu-backed) Congress and the Muslim League seemed to offer little hope of getting a united India. Instead, the prospect of civil war seemed a real possibility. Moreover, far from pledging friendship within the Commonwealth, most Congress leaders talked of a mass insurrection which would expel Britain from India 'lock, stock and barrel'.

Attlee was anxious not to impose a settlement upon the Indian people and wanted the Indians to work out their own solution but this was easier said than done. In 1945 the British Viceroy Lord Wavell held a conference of Indian political leaders of all parties at Simla to see if some agreement could be reached. But Congress and Muslim League leaders could not agree and the Simla conference was soon adjourned. Bevin, who had some doubts about Labour policy, supported the idea of delaying independence for a few years to enable Britain to finance a development programme for India. This notion, however, was quickly abandoned because India would be suspicious of any delay and because Britain could not afford the expense given her own economic difficulties.

In March 1946 a Cabinet mission was sent to India and quickly concluded that the Indians were unlikely to reach agreement without active British assistance. In May 1946 the British mission, therefore, produced its own plan. This envisaged the eleven Indian provinces forming themselves into groups, thus enabling the Muslim provinces to cluster together into a kind of Pakistan without full sovereignty. An All-India federal government would control foreign policy, defence and communications, but provincial governments would deal with all other matters. It seemed for a time that this scheme might be accepted by both Congress and the Muslim League.

But Congress leaders raised a host of quibbles and in late July the Muslim League withdrew its support for the plan and called for 'direct action' to achieve a united Pakistan. This led to serious rioting in Calcutta in which thousands of people were killed. Inter-communal massacres spread across much of Northern India.

In December 1946 Wavell returned to Britain. He told the Cabinet that civil war between India's 255 million Hindus and 92 million Muslims might break out at any time and that Britain could not maintain control beyond March 1948, if indeed as long as that. He suggested that the position might prove different if Britain declared its intention to remain in India for a further fifteen years and to reinforce its army by a further 4 or 5 divisions. Given the promises of the Labour government, this was out of the question. The worsening economic situation in Britain in 1946-7 played a part in encouraging the government to force the pace. Attlee favoured issuing an announcement to the effect that Britain proposed to transfer power in India not later than the following year. This was strongly opposed by Wavell. There was also disagreement about the manner in which British withdrawal should take place. Wavell thought it should be planned on the lines of a military evacuation from hostile territory. The Cabinet was convinced that the results of such a policy, pulling out as if driven out, would be appalling for India and Britain alike. Attlee believed that power could still be transferred in an orderly and even a friendly manner.

Attlee now took two vital initiatives. In February 1947 he publicly announced that Britain would leave India, come what may, no later than June 1948. He also dismissed Wavell who was replaced as Viceroy by Lord Mountbatten, formerly Supreme Allied Commander in South-East Asia. Mountbatten, prior to accepting the post, asked for and received power to make his own decisions on the spot. He arrived in India in March 1947 still hopeful that a settlement might be achieved which would preserve Indian unity.

However, Mountbatten quickly concluded that partition was the only answer: the alternative would be a dreadful civil war. Nehru, with whom Mountbatten had established a close rapport, gave his reluctant consent. This was perhaps Mountbatten's main achievement - although some historians consider that it was more the achievement of his wife, who established very intimate relations with the Congress leader! In June 1947 a final conference took place at which Nehru and Jinnah both gave their approval to Mountbatten's plan. Mountbatten, believing there was nothing to be said for further delay, determined to push the agreed plan through by mid-August 1947, abandoning in the process all hopes of an Anglo-Indian defence treaty. The plan provided for two dominions - India and Pakistan. Each Indian province would be free to join the dominion of its choice. Nothing was said about how the 565 Indian princely states were to be integrated into the two new dominions. Nor was it clear how the frontiers in the border areas were to be determined. What was certain was that partition would leave considerable religious minorities within both India and Pakistan. Nevertheless, the Indian Independence Bill was rushed through parliament, receiving royal assent on 15 August. The Raj was over and the future of India and Pakistan passed out of British control.

Most historians, echoing most contemporaries, think Britain had little option but to quit India (and many commend the speed at which the withdrawal occurred). The alternative would have been an intolerable burden on the British authorities in India and the possibility of civil war. There was the added danger that the situation might endanger Britain's relations with the USA and the Muslim world. Given the antagonism between Hindus and Muslims, by 1947 there seemed no alternative but partition. The decision of both India and Pakistan to remain within the Commonwealth was a symbol of the British government's success. Although a wave of massacres and counter-massacres followed Britain's withdrawal, Attlee insisted that Britain could not be blamed for the violence.

However, the critics of Attlee's policy had - and have - a case. Conservative leaders accused Attlee of betraying both India and Britain's own tradition. Britain had left India with little honour and dignity. The precipitate withdrawal probably contributed to the terrible communal violence (in which about half a million people probably died) which accompanied Britain's departure. From Britain's point of view, Attlee had achieved none of his initial aims. India was divided and Britain had no meaningful defence agreement with India or Pakistan, which were effectively totally independent. The gigantic precedent of India, the first non-white colonial territory to become independent, was likely to exert vital influence on the course of events in a great many other places. India was the most important of Britain's imperial possessions. Perhaps Churchill was right. If Britain lacked the will to rule in India, then her entire colonial empire would soon be lost.

With the loss of India, Britain had little further strategic interest in Burma and Ceylon. Much of Burma had been occupied by Japan in the Second World War and an embarrassing number of Burmese had collaborated with the Japanese. For a brief period after 1945 an attempt was made to restore British rule. But Attlee soon concluded that it was better to come to terms with the strong Burmese nationalist movement. By 1948 Burma had been granted full independence and had opted to leave the Commonwealth. Ceylon, which had made considerable progress to self-government before 1945, was given independence in February 1948. The country (which later changed it name to Sri Lanka) remained within the Commonwealth and agreed to a defence treaty with Britain.

9 The Middle East and Palestine

In 1945 Britain had a dominant presence in the Middle East. Britain had direct control over Malta and Cyprus. She had the right to keep troops in the Suez Canal Zone and shared responsibility with Egypt for the Sudan. She held Aden and effectively controlled most of the Sheikdoms along the southern coast of the Arabian peninsula and in the Persian Gulf. She had military bases in Iraq and had close ties with Jordan whose army was commanded by a British officer. She also held Palestine as a mandate from the United Nations. The only exception to British predominance was in Saudi Arabia, where American influence was growing, and in Iran, which Britain and the USSR had jointly occupied in 1941.

Bevin regarded the Middle East as of cardinal importance to the United Kingdom, first because of its oil reserves, most of which were controlled by British companies, and second because of the Suez Canal. He was determined that the area should remain a British sphere of influence and was particularly determined to keep Russian influence out. He hoped that co-operation with Middle East politicians would replace the coercive methods on which Britain had relied since 1940.

The main difficulties after 1945 were to come in Palestine, a British mandate since 1919 and a problem throughout the inter-war period. In 1917 the Balfour Declaration had promised to facilitate the establishment in Palestine of a national home for the Jewish people - although this was not supposed to prejudice the civil and religious rights of existing non-Jewish communities there. So-called Zionist Jews interpreted the Declaration as a promise to establish an independent Jewish state in Palestine. Throughout the 1920s and 1930s large numbers of Jews had settled in Palestine. (By 1939 they made up about 30 per cent of Palestine's population.) However, the Arabs who lived in Palestine had no wish to lose their land to Jewish settlers. There was trouble throughout the 1930s culminating in an Arab revolt in Palestine between 1936 and 1939. British officials had some sympathy with the Palestinian Arabs and did their best to limit Jewish immigration. In 1939 a White Paper proposed a total limit of 75,000 Jewish immigrants into Palestine over a 5 year period and also promised eventual independence to Palestine under Arab majority rule. It thus seemed as if the Zionist dream of a Jewish state was no longer attainable.

The Second World War made the Palestinian problem more insoluble. In 1945 there was tremendous sympathy for the survivors of the holocaust, especially in the USA. Moreover, by the summer of 1945 there were some 200,000 displaced Jews in Europe, many of whom wished to settle in Palestine. Within Palestine Britain had to face a well-organised and armed Jewish militia - the Haganah spearheaded by two terrorist organisations, the Stern Gang and the Irgun. Britain also had to satisfy the Palestinian Arabs who were determined to oppose the immigrant flood and the establishment of a Jewish state. Their cause was certain to be defended by all Arab states, particularly those bordering Palestine. On top of this, Britain had her own interests to protect. Given the uncertainty over the future of the Suez Canal, military chiefs argued that Palestine was important strategically and that Britain should continue to maintain a military presence there.

In 1945 most people expected that Attlee's government would support the Zionist cause. Labour had opposed the 1939 White Paper and a 1944 Labour policy statement had suggested that the Jews should be allowed to become the majority in Palestine. However, once in office, the Labour government quickly changed tack. The man most responsible for the change was Bevin. Within days of becoming Foreign Secretary he expressed doubts about large-scale Jewish immigration. Given the importance of Middle East oil, he had no wish to alienate the Arabs. Bevin's main aim, similar to the aim of British pre-war governments, was to find a compromise that would satisfy Jews and Arabs. The hopes of finding a compromise, despite Bevin's initial optimism (he said he would stake his political future on negotiating a settlement), were never high.

In September 1945 a Cabinet Committee supported Bevin and recommended a monthly quota of 1,500 Jewish immigrants to Palestine. This did not satisfy various Jewish agencies which demanded the immediate entry of 100,000 Jews. Within Palestine the Zionists resorted to more acts of terrorism and the British authorities found it increasingly difficult to maintain order. President Truman, courting the Jewish vote but also genuinely sympathetic to the Jewish cause, demanded continued immigration and an independent Jewish state (whilst refusing to assume any responsibilities for the situation in Palestine). Attlee tried to persuade the President that there were other places capable of receiving large numbers of Jews - without effect.

In November 1945 Bevin secured the appointment of an Anglo-American Committee to make recommendations on Palestine's future. Britain had hoped that the two issues - the future of Palestine and the settlement of European Jews - could both be studied. But the Americans would only agree to consider the problem of Jewish settlement within the specific context of Palestine. The Anglo-American Committee, reporting in May 1946, opposed the idea of partition but recommended the immediate admission of 100,000 Jewish immigrants. The report was immediately rejected both by Jewish and Arab leaders. British policy-makers disapproved of the immigrant recommendations because of the harm they would do to Anglo-Arab relations. Truman, however, immediately announced his support for the admittance of 100,000 immigrants. Attlee and Bevin were appalled. The Cabinet decided that it would only agree to this figure if illegal Jewish military organisations in Palestine were disbanded and if the USA would accept the responsibility with Britain for implementing the

Committee's recommendations. Neither conditions were satisfied.

Acts of terror increased. In July 1946 the King David Hotel in Jerusalem was blown up by Jewish terrorists, killing 91 people, many of whom were British. This event strengthened Britain's determination to oppose concessions to Jewish immigrants. Britain's main plan in the summer of 1946 was for Palestine to be divided into Arab and Jewish provinces under a central administration presided over by a British High Commissioner. But this plan stood little chance of success. President Truman opposed it as did Arabs and Jews and it proved impossible to get together a Conference in London to discuss the scheme.

The low point in Anglo-American relations came in October 1946 when Truman reaffirmed his support for the immediate admission of 100,000 Jewish immigrants. Attlee sent a terse reproof to the President. In January 1947 a new round of talks began. By now Truman had accepted the idea of partition, but Bevin, aware that the Arabs were totally opposed to a Jewish state in any part of Palestine and aware that neither side would accept boundaries agreeable to the other, opposed the idea. There seemed no room for compromise and Bevin admitted to being 'at the end of my tether'.

By early 1947 100,000 men, one tenth of Britain's armed forces, occupied a territory the size of Wales - the equivalent of one soldier for every 18 inhabitants - at an annual cost of £40 million. But the British authorities were still unable to keep order in the face of Jewish resistance. Even Churchill could see no merit in hanging on in Palestine. The conscript soldiers who were there 'might well be at home strengthening our depleted industry', he told the Commons. 'What are they doing there? What good are we getting out of it?'

In February 1947, as the economic situation in Britain worsened, Bevin referred the Palestine problem back to the United Nations. This was a gamble as much as an admission of defeat. Bevin believed that the United Nations would fail to come up with a practical solution and that this would strengthen Britain's hand and reduce, if not end, American and other international criticism.

Britain continued to lose the world-wide propaganda war. In July 1947 the ship Exodus carrying 4,500 illegal refugees was boarded by the Royal Navy off Palestine and forced to turn back. Britain decided to send the refugees to Hamburg, part of the British zone in Germany, an insensitive decision which provided the Zionist cause with a propaganda coup.

The United Nations special committee on Palestine finally reported in September 1947. It concluded that the British mandate should end and that independence should be granted to Palestine as soon as possible. By seven votes to four the committee advocated partition, with Jerusalem remaining under the control of the United Nations. The proposed Jewish state was to cover 55 per cent of the area of Palestine, although the Jews only numbered one third of the population. 150,000

Jewish immigrants were to be admitted over the two year period during which British responsibility as a mandatory power would continue to be exercised.

Bevin was outraged by the United Nations proposals, claiming them to be 'manifestly unjust to the Arabs' and predicting an Arab rising in Palestine. But in November 1947 the report was carried by 33 votes to 13. Britain abstained. In December the British government declared it had no intention of implementing a settlement with which it so strongly disagreed and announced that Britain would quit Palestine within six months.

Despite American pressure to stay, Bevin adhered rigidly to his determination to leave Palestine and by May 1948 most British troops had departed. The state of Israel was proclaimed and immediately recognised by the USA. It was soon invaded by the neighbouring Arab states - Egypt, Transjordan, Lebanon, Syria and Iraq. However, by January 1949, against the odds (and British expectations) the Israelis pushed back the invaders and actually gained territory. Therefore the United Nations partition plan did not come into effect and many Palestinian Arabs found themselves within the new state of Israel. Britain gave a somewhat belated recognition to Israel in January 1949.

Some historians have attributed the tragedy of the Palestine situation to British misrule. Many Arabs blame Britain for allowing Jewish immigrants into Palestine in the first place. Jews, on the other hand, have sometimes accused Bevin of being anti-semitic and opposing the creation of Israel. It is certainly possible to make out a strong case against the 1917 Balfour Declaration which encouraged Jews to settle in Palestine. But this was a decision made many years before Attlee's government came to power. Arguably Attlee and Bevin inherited an impossible situation in 1945. Bevin did his best to reconcile the irreconcilable, but given the intransigences of both sides, compromise proved to be an impossible goal. Britain can be accused of abdicating her responsibilities in Palestine in 1948 - but by then over 300 British lives had been lost and £100 million had been spent in a vain attempt to quell the forces of Jewish and Arab nationalism. It is possibly fairer to blame the USA (as Bevin himself did) for promoting the Zionist cause and not accepting more responsibility in Palestine. To charge Bevin with being anti-semitic is unfair. He hoped to treat Arab and Jew alike. But he was also determined to preserve Britain's influence in the Middle East. A pro-Jewish policy in Palestine would have seriously damaged Britain's standing among all Arabs in the region.

Although Britain emerged with no great credit from the Palestine debacle, at least Bevin had managed to isolate Palestine from the overall development of Anglo-American relations, and Britain continued to dominate the Middle East and retain alliances with many Arab states.

10 Conclusion

In 1945 the Labour government had hoped for an era of peace and prosperity and intended to preserve Britain's world power status. By 1948 these hopes had been rudely shattered. Mutual distrust and antipathy dominated the relations between the USSR and the West. Britain had stumbled from one economic crisis to another and by 1948 it was clear that Britain was no longer in the same superpower league as the USA and the USSR.

Given this situation it was - and still is - easy to criticise Labour's external policy-making. 'It is with deep grief I watch the clattering down of the British Empire with all its glories', Churchill told the Commons in March 1947. 'Scuttle, everywhere is the order of the day'. Many on the left were more critical of Britain's increasingly subservient relationship to the USA and were disappointed that Britain had failed to offer a distinctive ideology to the world, a middle way between Soviet communism and American capitalism. Modern historians (of both left- and right-wing views) tend to criticise Labour for not cutting Britain's overseas commitments.

There is some truth in all these charges. However, many historians are convinced that, given the massive problems that Britain faced, Attlee and Bevin deserve more praise than blame. Economic weakness was the major problem. Not for nothing did Bevin tell British miners to give him another million tons of coal and he would give them a new foreign policy! The accusation of scuttle can be seen as unfair. Bevin was not one to relinquish voluntarily one ounce of British power. Britain had little option but to accept Indian independence and even Churchill supported withdrawal from Palestine. Given Britain's economic position, the idea that Britain might somehow become a 'third force' was little more than a pipedream. The notion that Britain could or should somehow stand between the USA and the USSR and play off one against the other was similarly unrealistic. Even a Labour government was far closer to the USA than to the totalitarian USSR. Arguably Bevin's greatest achievement was to help persuade the USA that she should take over much of Britain's world policeman role. Far from being an American satellite, it can be claimed that Britain persuaded the USA to act as she wanted in 1947-8.

Finally the Labour government had little option but to accept Britain's world-wide commitments. For any British government to have embarked upon a policy of precipitate withdrawal would have been regarded as defeatist and as a premature act of abdication which would almost certainly have resulted in regional chaos, communist gains, and disastrous economic consequences for Britain.

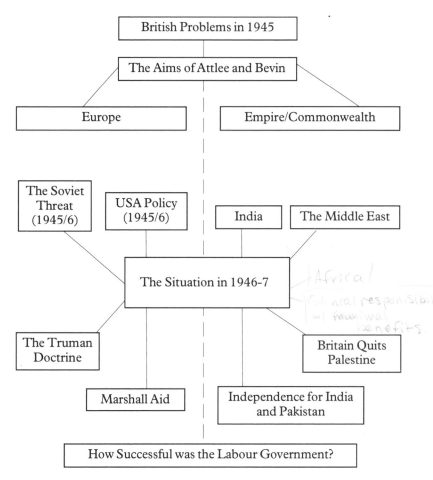

Summary - Post-War Problems, 1945-8

***Making notes on** 'Post-War Problems, 1945-8'*

This chapter is designed to show what problems Attlee's government faced immediately after the war and how it attempted to tackle them. The headings and sub-headings used in the chapter should help you to organise the material and compile a detailed summary of the main events 1945-8. As in the previous chapter, you should try to expand the final section ('Conclusion') by attempting to formulate your own judgements about the success or failure of British external policy in this period. As a means of doing this, you might briefly answer the following

questions:
1   What were the aims of Attlee and Bevin and how successful were
    they in achieving them?
2   Did the Labour government have any option but to pursue the
    policies it did with regard to the USSR, the USA, India and
    Palestine?
3   To what extent was Britain to blame for the start of the Cold
    War?

Source-based questions on 'Post-War Problems, 1945-8'

1 Churchill's Fulton speech, 1946
Read Churchill's speech on page 39. Answer the following questions:
a) What did Churchill mean by the term the 'iron curtain'? (2 marks)
b) Churchill mentions 10 capitals. Link the capitals to European
    countries. (5 marks)
c) What did Churchill mean by the term the 'fifth column'? (3 marks)
d) Why was Churchill convinced that there was no real danger of war?
    (3 marks)
e) What did Churchill propose should be the Anglo-American
    response to the Russian threat? (3 marks)
f) What do you think were Churchill's motives for making the speech?
    (4 marks)
g) In what ways might Attlee and Bevin have agreed or disagreed with
    the main ideas expressed by Churchill? (5 marks)

2 The Russian threat 1947
Examine the cartoons on pages 40 and 45. Answer the following
questions:
a) What point is 'The Truman Line' cartoon trying to make? (5 marks)
b) What point is Low's cartoon trying to make? (5 marks)
c) Comment on the portrait on the right hand side of the Low cartoon.
    (3 marks)
d) Which of the countries in Low's cartoon were largely under
    Communist control by the end of 1947? (4 marks)
e) On what points - if any - do the two cartoons agree? (3 marks)

CHAPTER 4

Labour Foreign and Imperial Policy, 1948-51

1 Introduction

1947 had been a dramatic year in Britain's external relations. Key decisions - particularly the abandonment of Greece, India and Palestine - had been taken which made a decisive break with the past and which laid the foundations upon which future governments would have to build. However, policy-makers still had some room for manoeuvre. They could look to Britain's imperial links, they could try and establish closer European connections, or they could link Britain even closer to the USA. Bevin had few doubts about the course he thought Britain should take. He remained convinced that the USSR posed the main threat to Britain. In consequence, his aim was to ensure that the USA would go beyond the Truman Doctrine and Marshall Aid and fully commit itself to Western Europe's defence. The deteriorating international situation ensured that Bevin was in a strong position to achieve his main aim.

2 The Communist Threat in 1948

By the start of 1948 relations between the West and Russia were severely strained. There was deadlock over Germany and the Stalinisation of Eastern Europe gathered pace. In January 1948 Attlee told the nation in a radio broadcast that:

> Soviet Communism pursues a policy of imperialism in a new form - ideological, economic and strategic - which threatens the welfare and way of life of the other nations of Europe.

Bevin was even more convinced that Soviet expansion was a real danger. 'It has', he said, 'become a matter of the defence of western civilisation'.

In February 1948 Soviet-supported communists seized power in Czechoslovakia, the last outpost of democracy in Eastern Europe. The new Czech communist government announced that Jan Masaryk, the pro-Western Foreign Minister, had committed suicide by leaping from his bathroom window. (It is now established, as many suspected at the time, that he did not jump but was pushed to his death by the communist secret police.) Events in Czechoslovakia helped silence the left-wing critics of Bevin's policy.

In the spring of 1948 it seemed possible that Russia might move against Norway. The following aide-memoire from Bevin to the American Secretary of State George Marshall in March 1948 indicates the British Foreign Secretary's thinking.

1 Mr Bevin considers that the most effective steps would be to take
very early steps before Norway goes under, to conclude ... a
regional Atlantic Approaches Pact of Mutual Assistance, in which
all the countries directly threatened by a Russian move to the
5 Atlantic could participate ... We could at once inspire the
necessary confidence to consolidate the West against Soviet
infiltration and at the same time inspire the Soviet Government
with enough respect for the West to remove temptation from them
10 and ensure a long period of peace. The alternative is to repeat our
experience with Hitler.

In the event the Soviet threat to Norway did not materialise. Nor did the
USA fully commit itself to defend Western Europe. Aware that America
was only likely to make a commitment to defend Europe if Europeans
showed that they were ready to help themselves, Britain (in March
1948) signed the Brussels Treaty with France and the Benelux countries
(Belgium, Holland and Luxembourg). The five countries pledged
themselves to come to the aid of any of their number which were
attacked. Joint planning and joint military exercises were soon
underway. Bevin hoped that the Brussels Treaty might thus be a 'sprat'
to catch the American 'mackerel'.

3 The Berlin Air Lift, 1948-9

By 1948 it was clear that there was no prospect of any agreement
between Russia and the West over Germany. In the Soviet zone
communist influence grew stronger while the British and American
zones to a large extent amalgamated. Despite lingering suspicion of
Germany, Britain came to accept the American view that Europe would
not fully recover from the effects of war until West Germany had
recovered economically. In consequence, the Western powers felt that,
rather than leave the German problem in limbo, they would be better
making their own arrangements on the assumption that the division of
Germany was permanent. By mid-June 1948 plans for the establishment
of a West German Federal Republic were underway, including a
proposal to introduce a new currency.

Russia now intervened. Hoping to pressurise the West into
abandoning the creation of a West German state, the Russians (in late
June 1948) imposed a blockade on all rail and road routes to Berlin,
under 4-power occupation but deep within the Soviet zone of Germany.
It seemed certain that West Berlin, with some 2,500,000 people and
only enough food for 36 days, would be starved into submission.

The Berlin crisis had not been anticipated in either the USA and
Britain but it was immediately clear to both Western powers that the

Russian move must not go unchallenged. If West Berlin was lost, the whole of West Germany might follow. President Truman, against the advice of Churchill, decided not to issue nuclear threats. Instead the USA started to put together a military convoy which would force its way down the autobahn to Berlin. Bevin, fearing war, took up the idea of British officials in Berlin and proposed an airlift to keep West Berlin supplied. The Americans were quickly won over to this idea, judging that whereas Russia might oppose an armed convoy, she would not risk shooting down transport planes.

The joint Anglo-American air-lift was a remarkable achievement. Western aircraft, landing at 3 minute intervals, succeeded in supplying West Berlin for eleven months. (Britain provided one third of the flights, one quarter of the supplies and the greater part of the ground organisation.) In May 1949 the USSR accepted defeat and abandoned the blockade. Later that summer the Federal Republic of Germany, made up of the British, American and French zones came into existence.

The Berlin crisis had an important result for Britain. American B-29 strategic bombers arrived in Britain in July 1948. Based in East Anglia, they were within striking distance of Moscow. Contrary to the impression (deliberately) conveyed at the time, the B-29s did not at first have nuclear capability. But by 1949 some did carry atomic bombs. The American nuclear presence on British soil was a huge step for both nations. A Cabinet Committee (not parliament) approved the arrival of the B-29s, convinced that American bases in Britain were essential and would help keep the USA firmly committed to Europe. However, the question of who precisely controlled the US bombers ran on for the next three years. Britain hoped (without success) to get a guarantee that the USA would not launch a nuclear strike from Britain without Britain's permission.

4 NATO

The Berlin crisis enabled Bevin to achieve his aim of ensuring that the USA would commit itself to the defence of Europe. By the summer of 1948 the Truman administration was ready to support such a policy and Congress permitted serious negotiations to start. The re-election of Truman in the 1948 presidential election helped the negotiations. The result - in April 1949 - was the North Atlantic Treaty. This pledged America, Britain and 10 other nations (France, Belgium, the Netherlands, Luxemburg, Italy, Norway, Denmark, Iceland, Portugal and Canada) to treat an attack on one as an attack on all. The most crucial part of the Treaty was Article 5:

1 The Parties agree that an armed attack against one or more of them in Europe or North America shall be considered an attack against all of them and consequently agree that, if such an armed attack

COME INTO THE GARDEN, CLEM

Vicky cartoon, drawn for the News Chronicle, *but unpublished*

David Low cartoon, Daily Herald, *12 January 1951*

occurs, each of them, in exercise of the right of individual or
5 collective self-defence recognised by Article 51 of the United
Nations Charter, will assist the party or parties so attacked by
taking forthwith, individually and in concert with the other parties,
such action as may be deemed necessary, including the use of
10 armed force, to restore and maintain the security of the North
Atlantic area.

Some critics complained at the time that the tortuous wording of Article
5 meant that the Treaty in fact lacked teeth. Certainly the wording did
leave the USA (and the other signatories) in principle free to choose
whether to go to war or not. In 1949 the North Atlantic Treaty was
perhaps more a loose mutual defence pact than a tight military alliance.
Nevertheless it was vitally important. It was America's first ever
peacetime alliance and put an American military-security roof over
Western Europe. In January 1950 the North Atlantic Treaty
Organisation (NATO) was officially instituted with a permanent
command structure. Decisions on military strategy were to be
collectively determined. Each member state would delegate part of its
military forces for permanent NATO duties. After 1949 Britain's armed
forces were at NATO's disposal and British diplomacy was conducted
with careful regard to the views of her NATO partners, especially those
of America, by far the most powerful member of the organisation.

5 The Communist Threat, 1949-50

Faced with the huge superiority of Soviet forces in Europe (where 175
Soviet divisions faced 14 Western divisions), Attlee's government felt it
had no option but to maintain Britain's defences. Work on the British
atomic bomb continued, effectively screened from the public, from
parliament and even from the Cabinet. Britain's conventional forces
were the main topic of debate, especially the continuation of
conscription. The National Service Bill of March 1947 which called up
men for 18 months led to the most serious Labour rebellion during
Attlee's premiership. The government considered reducing the length of
the call-up period to 12 months but the threat of revolt by the Army
Chiefs of Staff ensured that the original terms of the bill survived and the
Act came into force in 1949.

In 1949 the communist threat suddenly increased. Until 1949 the
West - or more accurately the USA - had the strength to neutralise the
superiority of Soviet ground forces simply because it had the atomic
bomb. In August 1949, however, the Russians tested their own atomic
bomb. This had been anticipated but its actual development was ahead
of Western expectations.

To make matters worse, in September 1949 Chinese communist
forces led by Mao Tse-tung came to power after defeating the Chinese

Nationalists. The Nationalist leader Chiang Kai-shek retreated to the island of Taiwan. Britain and the USA were divided in their attitudes to the new China. The USA refused to recognise the new communist government and denied it the right to representation at the United Nations. But Bevin, who was concerned for the British colony of Hong Kong and for British business interests in China, was anxious to retain contacts with China. (He also believed this was the best way to reduce Russian influence in China.) In January 1950, therefore, Britain recognised the People's Republic of China to the chagrin of many Americans who thought Britain was going 'soft' on communism. In an attempt to keep the USA happy Britain accepted that the Chinese Nationalist regime in Taiwan should occupy China's seat on the Security Council of the United Nations.

But the fact remained that by 1950 the world's largest country (the USSR) and the world's most populous country (China) were both communist. Most Americans assumed that the two communist powers would work together in an attempt to bring about world-wide communist revolution. They over-looked the fact that the USSR and China had their own serious disagreements which the West, in time, might be able to exploit. Nevertheless the notion of a communist monolith was easy to accept in 1950, particularly as Russia and China now signed a treaty of friendship. Developments in Korea seemed to confirm the communist menace.

6 Korea

In 1945 Korea, ruled by Japan for most of the twentieth century, was divided into two zones: the area north of the 38th parallel was to be under Russian control; and the area south of the line was to be under American control. It had not been intended that this should be a permanent division but it soon became clear that no agreement over Korea's future was likely. After 1947 the two parts of Korea were organised under separate civil administrations, each claiming to be the sole lawful government of the whole country. In 1949 Russian and American troops withdrew from North and South Korea respectively, but the Russians left behind many military advisers.

In June 1950 North Korea attacked South Korea, taking both the South Koreans and the Americans completely by surprise. The Americans were convinced that this aggression was part of a vast Russian plan to advance the cause of communism. The British Foreign Office had no doubt that the Russians had connived at, even if they had not fully instigated, the North Korean attack. British policy-makers feared that Stalin had planned the invasion in order to divert American attention to Asia so that he would be in a strong position to put pressure on Western Europe.

At first it seemed as if North Korea's more numerous and better equipped forces would achieve total victory. Although historians still debate the extent to which the USSR had actually promoted the attack, there is, and was, no doubt that victory for North Korea would constitute a very important moral triumph for communism and the USSR. President Truman, in consequence, was determined to support South Korea.

Attlee's government also supported firm action. The United Nations Security Council was called into special session. By a lucky chance Russia was boycotting the United Nations in protest at the Security Council's refusal to displace Nationalist China in favour of Red China. Truman, therefore, was able to secure unanimous support for a resolution calling on all members to assist in compelling North Korea to withdraw its forces. In consequence the force that was sent to Korea, although largely American, was fighting under a United Nations (UN) banner. The British government, as a loyal ally of the USA and a dutiful member of the UN, accelerated re-armament, extended conscription to two years and sent British forces to Korea. Although the British military contribution was tiny compared with that of the USA, Britain did provide substantial air and naval support.

UN forces led by the American General, Douglas MacArthur, were initially highly successful. They forced back the North Koreans and by the end of September had reached the 38th parallel and were in a position to invade North Korea. Neither the USA nor Britain were prepared at this stage merely to see the restoration of the status quo. Both countries had no doubt that North Korea should be punished for its aggression. Although Britain (rather more than America) was concerned at the prospect of Chinese intervention, there seemed to be an excellent opportunity to roll back communism. In early October UN forces crossed the 38th parallel.

By November 1950, UN troops had occupied two thirds of North Korea and had reached the Yalu River, the frontier between North Korea and China. Britain continued to maintain that the risk of hostilities from China would be less if China was admitted to the UN. This carried no weight with the Americans who similarly ignored warnings from the Indian leader Nehru that the Chinese were about to intervene. Chinese intervention came at the end of November 1950. UN forces, taken totally by surprise, were soon in headlong retreat and Chinese forces drove deep into South Korea, threatening to drive UN forces out of the country.

On 30 November Truman, speaking at a Press Conference, unwittingly gave the impression that the US was considering using nuclear weapons against China. This caused such anxiety in Britain that Attlee flew to America to see Truman. Truman quickly reassured Attlee that the US had no intention of using atomic bombs. A relieved Attlee encouraged Truman to keep the war limited to the Korean peninsula in the face of strong American pressure to bomb the Chinese mainland.

Early in 1951 UN forces held up and then drove the communists back to the 38th parallel. Rather than push further north, the UN forces now took up defensive positions close to the 38th parallel and the military position became something of a stalemate. Truman, therefore, was not faced with the terrible dilemma of either accepting a humiliating defeat whose world-wide consequences could prove shattering, or involving men and resources to an almost unlimited extent in the defence of Korea. However, he did face other problems. General MacArthur, who favoured an all-out war against China, disagreed publicly with Truman over the UN's defensive strategy. In April 1951 Truman, determined not to be forced into the dangers of a global conflict by an insubordinate soldier, removed MacArthur from his command. Peace negotiations were begun but failed to reach a conclusion and the Korean war was to drag on until 1953. However, Korea was no longer quite so much the centre of world attention or the fuse which might detonate World War Three. It was clear by 1951 that South Korea had been saved.

After America, Britain had sent the largest contingent of troops to Korea. British casualties (4,000 wounded: 700 killed) were small compared with those of the USA (105,000 wounded: 33,000 killed). But the British troops had fought well, and without Britain's participation in Korea it would have been hard to claim that the miscellaneous contingents supporting South Korea were a credible UN, as opposed to an American, force.

The USA and Britain had stood firm and made the point that aggression did not pay. From Britain's point of view the Korean war had some positive effects. It did much to strengthen NATO. After 1950 the USA expanded both its conventional forces and its nuclear arsenal and was fully committed to the defence of Europe. The Korean war also helped strengthen Britain's special relationship with the USA. Nevertheless the war did have serious economic consequences for Britain.

7 British Economic Problems

The American loan of 1945 and Marshall Aid after 1948 had helped prop up Britain's economy. By 1948 Britain's trade was again in balance, thanks to a remarkable surge in exports. However, the pound remained over-valued against the dollar and Britain remained desperately short of dollars and gold reserves. In September 1949 the government, after intense pressure on the foreign exchanges, devalued the pound from $4.03 to $2.80. This decision, taken without prior consultation with European or Commonwealth countries, was a blow to Britain's prestige. Nevertheless, devaluation did put the pound in a more realistic balance with the dollar and enhanced Britain's competitive position abroad.

However, the Korean war gave a serious jolt to Britain's economic recovery. Attlee's government, fearful of Soviet aggression in Europe, and under pressure from the USA, believed it had no option but to strengthen Britain's defences. Between June 1950 and January 1951 the defence budget nearly doubled. Rearmament led to a cut in Britain's export drive and to a new balance of payments crisis as defence contractors competed with the manufacturers of civilian goods for skilled labour, machine tools and raw materials. In addition, the government was forced to raise taxes at home. The decision to charge National Health Service patients half the costs of spectacles and dentures led to the resignation from the Cabinet of the Minister of Labour Aneurin Bevan, who complained that Britain had allowed herself 'to be dragged too far behind the wheels of American diplomacy'.

Some historians think Britain was on the verge of an economic miracle in 1950 which would have enabled her to have recovered her export markets to the point that Germany and Japan would not have been able to challenge her. This is simply conjecture. What is certain, however, is that Britain by 1951 was spending a higher percentage of its national income on defence than any of its European NATO allies. There seems little doubt that as a result of the Korean war, British export markets became increasingly vulnerable. While Britain was building tanks and planes, Germany and Japan were building the machinery with which they were to achieve their later economic success.

8 European Integration

After 1945 some people believed there was a need for closer West European co-operation. The reasoning was simple. A co-operative effort might help Western Europe recover from the ravages of the Second World War, meet the threat from Russia, and prevent the likelihood of war between West European countries in the future. In September 1946 Winston Churchill at Zurich spoke of the need to create a kind of 'United States of Europe' and urged the creation of a Council of Europe. Churchill, it should be said, saw Britain as a sponsor rather than as a founding member of such a Council. Even so in January 1947 a United Europe Committee was set up in London with Churchill as Chairman. The aim of this body was the creation of a 'unified Europe'.

There were different views of what a 'unified Europe' should be like. Some wanted Europe's nation states to retain their separate identities but to agree to co-operate on trade and defence matters, through treaties and mutual agreements. Some supported the idea of common economic and defence policies and were prepared to accept the need for supra-national authorities to implement such policies. Very few envisaged a fully-fledged European government responsible to a sovereign European parliament.

Attlee's government, while not particularly enthusiastic about European unity, was not totally averse to the idea of a British-led

Western European bloc. Bevin was keen to establish closer relations with European countries, especially France. Although French political instability made it difficult to reach agreement, in March 1947 Britain and France did sign a defensive alliance - the Treaty of Dunkirk. The Treaty was important not so much for its terms (which pledged co-operation in the event of a future German attack!) but for Britain's willingness to enter into a formal commitment with another European country.

In January 1948 Bevin went further and proposed the notion of a 'Western Union' which would link European countries culturally, economically and in defence terms. However, his vague hopes of closer West European collaboration, based on inter-government co-operation, were difficult to translate into something substantial. The Organisation for European Economic Co-operation (OEEC), set up in April 1948 to administer Marshall Aid, was a more important step towards European economic co-operation.

However, links with the Commonwealth and with the USA meant far more to Attlee's government than ties with war-torn Europe. By the late 1940s the Empire/Commonwealth took nearly half Britain's exports, while Western Europe took only a quarter. Moreover, few, if any, Labour MPs supported the idea of Britain joining some kind of European federation and sacrificing British sovereignty. Their suspicion of European federalism was perhaps best expressed by Bevin: 'if you open that Pandora's Box you never know what Trojan 'orses will jump out'.

Bevin soon lost his enthusiasm for a 'Western Union'. In May 1948 a Congress at the Hague, presided over by Churchill, was boycotted by the Labour government (partly because Churchill chaired it!). This Congress advocated the creation of European Assembly to be chosen from the parliaments of the member states. Churchill and the Conservatives gave the (largely false) impression that they stood for a united Europe whereas the Labour Party did not.

Although Attlee's government opposed the creation of a European Assembly, in May 1949 a Council of Europe was created, consisting of a Ministerial Council and a 'Consultative Assembly', made up of delegates from the parliaments of the member states. These were to meet regularly to discuss matters of common interest but Britain ensured that neither body could do more than make recommendations. The Council of Europe, therefore, was simply a 'talking shop' and, from the Labour government's point of view, fairly harmless.

The creation of NATO was, on the surface, a move towards European integration in defence matters. However, Bevin saw NATO as a means of strengthening Europe's links with America rather than as a means of fostering European co-operation. The creation of NATO, therefore, is an indication that Britain regarded relations with America as more important than relations with Europe.

'Maps and Men', a Vicky cartoon, 19 June 1950

When the French sounded out the idea of an Anglo-French economic union in the spring of 1949, the French economic planning chief Jean Monnet received a polite brush-off from British officials. Rebuffed by Britain, Monnet, who had a vision of a united Europe to which everything, including national sovereignty, was subordinate, turned to the new West German state. In May 1950 the French Foreign Minister, Robert Schuman, launched Monnet's new plan for a European Coal and Steel Community (ECSC), centred on France and West Germany. Although both Monnet and Schuman were committed to the ideal of a federal Europe, they also realised that this would be a way of absorbing a potentially powerful Germany within a supra-national framework.

Fearing a hostile British reaction, Schuman first outlined his proposals to Acheson, the new American Secretary of State, and to Adenauer, the West German Chancellor. Only later in May was Britain asked formally if she would care to join France and Germany in creating the ECSC. The manner of the announcement of the plan was not calculated to win British support. Bevin, believing he was the victim of a diplomatic plot, was outraged and protested strongly at Britain's exclusion from the preliminary soundings. Negotiations between Monnet and leading British civil servants achieved nothing except to show how far apart the two sides were. The main sticking point was national sovereignty. The French were prepared to sacrifice some national sovereignty: the British were not. There was also concern that a European coal and steel pool would jeopardise the newly nationalised British coal and the soon to be nationalised British iron and steel industries. Attlee, therefore, told the Commons that the scheme would require detailed study.

France, aware that Britain was hedging, retained the diplomatic initiative and on 1 June 1950 invited Britain, Italy and the Benelux countries to join in ECSC negotiations. All the countries had to indicate their intentions of doing so by 8.00pm the following day, and all had to accept the principle of supra-national authority in advance. This invitation-cum-ultimatum found the British Cabinet dispersed and the issue was not judged important enough to warrant its recall. With Attlee and Cripps on holiday (ironically enough in France) and with Bevin ill, the final decision was taken by a 'rump' Cabinet on 2 June 1950. Herbert Morrison, effectively deputy Prime Minister, said that the Durham miners would not wear the scheme and turned down the invitation. His decision, approved by Attlee and Bevin who had no wish to be dictated to by France, was fully in line with the tenor of all official thinking since 1947. Consequently Britain stood aside from the negotiations which opened in Paris on 3 June and which led ultimately to the formation of the ESCS in April 1951, with France, West Germany, Italy, Belgium, Luxembourg and the Netherlands as its six founder members.

A leading Civil Servant, Edwin Plowden, who took part in Britain's response to the ECSC proposals, later said:

1 We were still thinking in terms of Britain, and of standing between
the United States and Western Europe and Russia and so on; as
being an independent great power ... I don't think ... that we really
believed in the vision he [Monnet] had of forming a nucleus
5 around which a new Europe could be built. After all, for I don't
know how many hundreds of years Britain had kept out of Europe.
And suddenly to ask it to change, to give up its external, its
worldwide role in order to join with a Europe which was down and
10 out at the time, required a vision which I'm quite sure I hadn't got,
and I doubt whether very many people in the United Kingdom
had. Some may now think they had, but I don't think they did.

Similar considerations dictated Britain's initially brusque reaction to the
Pleven plan of October 1950. This called for an integrated
multi-national European army responsible to a European Assembly and
European Defence Minister. This was an extension of Monnet's
supranationalist principles from economics to defence. But it was also a
way of responding to American demands for West German rearmament
and a way of trying to ease (particularly French) fears of such a process
so soon after the Second World War.

Attlee at first dismissed the Pleven plan as 'unworkable and
unsound'. However, by the autumn of 1951 the Labour government's
attitude had modified because of American support for the plan and
because it seemed the best way to placate Labour backbench opposition
to German rearmament. Even so Attlee's government made it clear that
Britain wished to be 'associated' rather than fully involved with
developments.

Some historians have contended that by giving priority to national
sovereignty and to Britain's overseas interests, Attlee's government
missed the European bus. Acheson, the American Secretary of State,
thought Britain's refusal to join the ECSC was 'the greatest mistake of
the post-war period'. By 1951 Britain was no longer taking part in the
process of European integration, still less leading it.

However, other historians are less critical of the Labour government.
They point out that until 1948 Britain was at least as European-minded
as France. Bevin, for example, had very much encouraged the
development of a common European military infrastructure. Moreover,
in 1950 there was ample justification for the British decision to place
strict limits on European economic integration which seemed
irreconcilable with Britain's special trading relations with the Empire/
Commonwealth. The latter produced the essential raw materials which
Europe could not. Few people in 1950 foresaw the great growth in trade
between the West European industrial nations or the limitations of
Britain's traditional markets. In fairness to Attlee it should also be

pointed out that aloofness, if not hostility, to 'Europeanism' was not confined to the Labour government. While Churchill talked somewhat vaguely of European unity, most Conservatives (and the British public as a whole) remained largely indifferent. It is doubtful if any British government at the time would or could have acted differently with regard to closer links with Europe.

9 Developing the Commonwealth

The abandonment of Palestine and the granting of independence to India, Pakistan, Ceylon and Burma in 1947-8 was not seen by the Labour government as the start of a general decolonisation process. In very few places did Britain face the kind of internal pressures that had driven her out of Palestine and the Indian sub-continent. Attlee's government was acutely aware that Britain's prosperity and her continued position as a great power very much depended on the Empire/Commonwealth. Many policy-makers still hoped that the Commonwealth would become a third force, balancing the power of the USSR and the USA. There was also a realisation that if Britain abandoned the territories she controlled this would simply create a power vacuum which the USSR might fill.

Of all the various states and territories that made up the Empire/Commonwealth, the self-governing dominions of Canada, Australia, New Zealand and South Africa, were regarded as Britain's most reliable friends, tied to Britain not just by common interests and political traditions but by deep emotional bonds of kith and kin. Before 1939 the dominions had been prepared to follow Britain's lead in international affairs and they had gone to war on Britain's side in 1939.

Immediately after the war hopes that the partnership between Britain and the dominions could be fashioned into a much closer grouping with a common foreign policy and an integrated defence, soon collapsed. In fact it became more and more obvious that the dominions (now called Commonwealth countries) had their own interests and were prepared to assert their separate identities. Moreover, the dominions (like Britain herself) looked increasingly to the USA for security.

Although the old relationship between Britain and the 'white' dominions was changing, the Labour government was hopeful of building (from ex-colonial territories) a 'New' Commonwealth - a world-wide association of free, independent states - which would transcend race, colour and creed. The Commonwealth was seen as a unique experiment without precedent in history and full of promise for the future. It was easy to believe it would serve as an effective vehicle of British influence and that the new dominions would become like the old.

However, the old reliance on kith, kin and common culture as the invisible cement of the British-dominion relationship was put in doubt by the new Asian members of the Commonwealth. India, Pakistan and

Ceylon did not share the enthusiasm of the white dominions for the great power pretensions of Britain, still less their support for British colonial rule. The New Commonwealth was thus far less a club than the old. It enjoyed no natural unity and its members had little in common with each other. In addition, the talk of racial partnership as a central purpose of the New Commonwealth had little appeal to some of the older Commonwealth countries, especially South Africa. The Nationalist Government, which came to power in 1948 with the overwhelming support of the Boers, supported a policy of apartheid. Given South Africa's strategic and economic importance (it was a major source of uranium and gold), Attlee's government toned down its criticism of Nationalist policies. Even so South Africa's apartheid policies remained an embarrassment for Britain and at odds with the idea of the New Commonwealth.

In 1948-9 there seemed a danger that the New Commonwealth would collapse. Before 1948 dominion countries had been required to recognise the British Crown as their own head of state. In 1947 and 1948 Britain had made no effort to bend the rules to allow either Eire or Burma to become republics and stay within the Commonwealth. India's determination to become a republic in 1948-9, however, was a cause of major concern. India, a potentially vast trading partner and a seemingly vital ally in a continent where communist influence was advancing rapidly, was far more important than Burma or Eire. A compromise was finally worked out whereby republican India would remain within the Commonwealth, accepting the British monarch as 'Head of the Commonwealth' rather than as Head of the Indian State. This formula was accepted in April 1949 by a Commonwealth Prime Ministers' Conference.

10 The Sterling Area

Before 1945 British economic power had been an important foundation of the Empire/Commonwealth. However, the Second World War greatly weakened Britain's power as a trading nation, and by 1945 Britain no longer had an abundance of capital. There was thus a likelihood that the countries within the British imperial system which were free to do so would look to the USA for economic partnership. The unfree British dependencies, on the other hand, might well rebel against a colonial system that offered few economic benefits.

Strangely, however, Britain's post-war economic weakness served to reinforce Commonwealth solidarity in trade and finance. Almost all the dominions (and several independent countries such as Iraq) used the British pound sterling as the basis of their currency and banked their overseas earnings in London. The threat of the collapse of the pound in 1947 threatened them all with bankruptcy. Britain, moreover, remained the most important market for most members of the Sterling Area and the prospect of finding alternative markets for their primary products was poor. They seemed, therefore, to have little option but to sink or swim with Britain. Various measures, agreed to in 1947, tied the independent members of the Sterling Area far more closely than before 1939 to a common trade policy, limited their rights over their own credit and obliged them to purchase more of their imports from Britain. The Sterling Area, therefore, became a closed economic bloc in a way that the Empire had never been even at its height! With 25 per cent of the world's population and 25 per cent of its trade, the Sterling Area far exceeded its main rival, the dollar area. The perpetuation of this closely integrated trading and currency bloc was a central aim of British policy.

11 Developing the Colonies

In 1945 Britain still controlled a host of colonial territories, particularly in Africa. Before 1939 relatively little had been done in most of the colonies to encourage political independence. It was generally assumed that British rule would continue indefinitely. Little had also been done to promote economic or social reform. Few colonies experienced much in the way of economic prosperity.

For many years Labour politicians had talked in vague terms of 'developing' the colonies should a Labour government ever come to power. But most had little idea of what development should take place or how it should be done. Nevertheless, Arthur Creech-Jones, Attlee's Colonial Secretary, determined to aid Britain's colonies. He believed that Britain must act as a benevolent trustee for colonial peoples, ensuring they were not abused or exploited by white settlers or British capitalists. He regarded colonial economic and social development as the crucial pre-condition for progress to self-government. A Colonial Development and Welfare Act passed in 1945 allocated £120 million over 10 years to assist the colonies' development. A 1948 Act established the Colonial Development Corporation and the Overseas Food Corporation to improve living standards in the colonies.

By the late 1940s the Labour government claimed that it had abolished the old type of capitalist imperialism. However, the truth was somewhat different. Far from helping the colonies' economic development, Britain actually exploited her colonies for all they were worth, restricting investment, controlling their trade and the prices of their main commodities, and also rationing the goods they could purchase from Britain. The Labour government's main concern after 1945 was to earn dollars by export, then to satisfy British consumers and manufacturers. The colonies came very low on the list of priorities. Between 1945 and 1951 the colonies were forced to lend Britain far more money than Britain actually invested in the colonies. Arguably Attlee's government, for all its fine words, allowed the British dependencies to be exploited more than at any time since overseas colonies were established.

In Africa Britain embarked on what has been called a 'second colonial occupation'. Anxious to develop colonial economies as rapidly as possible to provide Britain with urgently needed raw materials, colonial governments interfered in all areas of economic life and scores of zealous British experts descended on Africa with schemes for agricultural improvement. The best known example of government intervention was the East African Groundnut Scheme. Launched in 1946 in an attempt to reduce the deficit of oils and fats in Britain (rather than to help East Africa), the scheme (which had cost the British taxpayer £36 million) by 1949 had come to nothing, providing neither margarine for Britain nor employment for Africans. This example of spectacular economic mismanagement was far from being an isolated one. The British government's enthusiasm for change also upset many of the local vested interests on whose support British colonial government depended. The weight of colonial rule seemed to be growing heavier and this led to increased resentment and uncertainty.

In 1948 riots in Accra convinced the British government that the Gold Coast (modern Ghana) was near to revolution. Britain, therefore, decided to give the Gold Coast Africans more say in the control of policy. Some see this as the starting point of a general process of rapid decolonisation in Africa. If power was devolved to Africans in one colony, there was no reason why this should not happen elsewhere. Nigerians, aware of the situation in Ghana, soon pressed (successfully) for more political participation. However, Attlee's government believed that the Gold Coast and Nigeria were special cases, and most experts thought that it would be many years before even these two countries had full responsible government and even longer before they were given full independence.

Nevertheless, Britain's deliberate encouragement of democratic politics presented African politicians with opportunities they could use to good effect. The Labour government, therefore, can be accused of fashioning a rod for Britain's own back. Whether intentionally or unintentionally, Attlee's government helped create the conditions in which colonial politicians would have the means to organise on a large scale and ultimately drive out British rule. In Labour's defence, however, it can also be claimed that the move towards African independence was gradually gathering momentum and there was little any British government could - or should - have done to prevent it.

12 Malaya and South East Asia

Even after 1947 Britain still had some interest in South East Asia, especially in Malaya. In 1945 the Malayan peninsula consisted of nine states, each ruled by a Sultan but under British protection, two British settlements, and Singapore. The population was multi-racial: mostly Malays and Chinese in roughly equal numbers but with Indians and Europeans as well. The area was vital economically because it produced one third of the world's tin and huge amounts of rubber, the bulk of both products being sold to the USA for vital dollars. Malaya was also important strategically, if the Indian Ocean was to remain a British lake.

In 1948 Britain, aiming to provide a stronger, more viable political unit, decided to group the states and settlements into the Federation of Malaya. To the consternation of the Malayan Chinese, it seemed that the Malays would dominate the new unit. Malayan communists, exploiting the Chinese community's disaffection and encouraged by events in China, stirred up strikes and violence against Britain. The situation became so serious that a state of emergency was declared and thousands of British troops were sent to Malaya. The guerilla war with the Malayan communists was to drag on until the late 1950s. Communist success would have had serious repercussions for British economic and strategic interests, and British withdrawal was not contemplated while the emergency lasted. Britain, helped by the fact that the majority of the population remained pro-British, dealt with the situation reasonably successfully, resettling all suspected communists in specially guarded villages. Not until 1953, however, did British forces really began to eliminate large numbers of guerilla bands.

Britain's ultimate success in Malaya contrasted with French problems in Indo-China and Dutch problems in the East Indies. However, the problems of fellow European colonial countries did have an impact on Britain's position in South-East Asia. Mao's triumph in China also added to Britain's discomfort. Although South-East Asia had been accepted as a European concern, Bevin realised that Britain needed American support if she was to contain the spread of communism in the region. After the start of the Korean War the USA did begin to intervene more, providing massive economic aid to the hard-pressed French in Indo-China.

Britain's abdication of power was evident with the formation of the ANZUS military pact between Australia, New Zealand and the USA in 1951. Significantly Britain was excluded. Although Attlee claimed that the pact was in line with the notion that individual Commonwealth countries should take the lead on behalf of the whole Commonwealth in areas where they were especially concerned, the ANZUS pact did seem to imply that the USA had taken over Britain's responsibilities in the Pacific.

13 The Middle East

Despite the abandonment of Palestine, Britain continued to exert considerable influence over the Middle East. Given that Britain's strong position in the area had been secured in order to defend the routes to

India, the loss of the Indian sub-continent perhaps ought to have led to a far-reaching re-examination of Britain's future in the Middle East. But Bevin continued to view the area as of vital importance strategically and economically, British companies controlling a significant part of the region's oil production.

On the whole Bevin tried to maintain British hegemony by co-operating with the Arab states in the region. He talked of 'a common basis of partnership' whereby Britain would offer investment and technical assistance in return for new treaties guaranteeing Britain's essential interests. Unfortunately Britain's weak economy made it hard for her to provide the Arab states with much in the way of economic help.

After 1947 Britain's main military centre in the Middle East was Egypt where the Suez Canal Zone formed a complex of bases in which nearly 40,000 troops were located in 1951. However, the Egyptians wanted British forces to quit Suez. Talks with Egypt over Suez and over the future of Sudan had been underway since 1945 but it proved impossible to reach an agreement on either issue. In April 1951 the Egyptian government demanded that British forces should be evacuated from the country within a year. In October 1951 Egypt formally abrogated the 1936 treaty which gave Britain the right to remain in the Suez Canal base. The Egyptian King Farouk also assumed the title of King of Sudan. These actions were clearly intended to heighten the Anglo-Egyptian dispute.

14 The End of Bevin and Attlee

The Labour Party won the February 1950 general election but with a majority of only 5 over all the other parties. This made it hard to govern. In March 1951 Bevin, the lynch-pin of government since 1945, resigned. He had suffered serious ill-health for much of 1950. He died in April 1951. He was succeeded as Foreign Secretary by Herbert Morrison. Although relations between Bevin and Morrison had been notoriously bad, Morrison had little chance in practice to depart from his predecessor's policies. Despite their differences, Morrison was a patriot in a similar mould to Bevin. He had little previous experience of foreign affairs and it was said of him that whereas Bevin could not pronounce the names of foreign places, Morrison did not know where they were.

Morrison's main concern was Iran, the largest oil-producing state in the Middle East and the chief source of British oil imports. The Anglo-Iranian Oil Company (in which the British government was a major shareholder), owned most of the Iranian oil fields and a huge refinery at Abadan. In April 1951 a new Iranian government, headed by Dr Mohammed Mossadiq, nationalised the Anglo-Iranian Company. Attlee's government, while not objecting to nationalisation in principle, was angry that the Iranians paid no compensation. Morrison (a conscientious objector in the First World War!) itched to use military force but without the Indian army Britain lacked ready manpower to intervene. There was also a risk that British intervention in southern Iran would prompt Russian action in northern Iran. The USA, fearing an anti-imperialist backlash and concerned at the prospect of Iran falling or swinging to the USSR, opposed the use of force. The USA also had some sympathy with the Iranians whom they saw as victims of British imperialism. Without American approval Attlee's government decided that it was in no position to undertake a major military operation. Instead it imposed a boycott of Iranian oil. The dispute was referred to the International Court at the Hague but this achieved nothing. The whole episode seemed an embarrassing exposure of Britain's weakness.

Attlee, faced with internal party divisions, a balance of payments crisis, and finding it hard to carry on business with so small a majority, decided to call a general election in October 1951. Foreign policy was an important issue in the election campaign. Winston Churchill, still the Conservative leader, exploited his reputation for statesmanship. Britain was still at war with North Korea and Churchill was a proven war leader. Churchill's charge of Labour neglecting Britain's national interests (especially in Iran) was countered by Labour accusing Churchill of 'war-mongering'. The Daily Mirror, suggesting that peace was not safe in Churchill's hands, ran a headline, 'Whose finger do you want on the trigger?' Churchill successfully sued the paper for libel but Labour's efforts to frighten the electorate possibly had some success. Labour did better than expected and actually won more votes than the Conservatives. But the Conservatives won more seats in the House of Commons and Churchill replaced Attlee as Prime Minister.

15 Conclusion

It is possible to praise Labour foreign and imperial policy in the period 1945-51. Some historians, such as Alan Bullock, regard Ernest Bevin as one of Britain's greatest Foreign Secretaries - a man with immense authority in Cabinet and Parliament, respected by most foreign diplomats, and with the courage to stand up for what he believed in. Arguably he achieved most of his aims. He can be seen as skilfully manoeuvering the USA into a position where it would face up to the very real Russian threat in Europe. The creation of NATO is often seen as Bevin's greatest achievement, serving its purpose for over 40 years and enabling Britain to exercise greater influence over American policy than would otherwise have been the case. Attlee's government can be credited with taking a number of hard but realistic decisions, including the production of the atom bomb and the sending of forces to Korea. Despite the loss of India, despite a succession of currency and trading crises, and the division of the world into two hostile camps, Britain in

1951 was still well ahead of all other states except the USSR and the USA in military, industrial and technological resources. She still dominated Africa and the Middle East, and the Indian Ocean remained a British lake. The Sterling Area guaranteed Britain a privileged market which insulated the British economy from foreign competition and meant there was no need to join a European federation.

However, it is also possible to be critical of Labour policy-making. Bevin's diplomatic skill should be viewed in context. Arguably the actions of Russia did more than astute British diplomacy to convince America of the need to intervene in Europe. Perhaps Bevin exaggerated the Russian threat and tied Britain too closely to the USA - so much so

	USA	USSR/ China	Europe	Empire/ Commonwealth		Other
1948	Marshall Aid	Czechoslovakia	Brussels Treaty	Burma and Eire left the Commonwealth		
	Berlin air lift	Berlin blockade	OEEC	Emergency in Malaya		
	B29s based in Britain		Hague Congress	Riots in Accra		
1949	NATO	End of Berlin blockade	Council of Europe	India became a republic		Britain devalued
		USSR tested an atom bomb	Creation of W. Germany			the pound
		China became Communist				
1950	Korean War		ESCS plan			General
		China intervened in Korea	Pleven plan			Election
1951	Korean War continued		Formation of ESCS	ANZUS Pact		Morrison replaces Bevin
						Iran nation- alised Anglo- Iranian oil
						General Election

Summary - Labour Foreign and Imperial Policy, 1948-51

that America was on top rather than on tap. As a result Britain was dragged into the Korean war. Moreover by 1949 Britain had become a front-line American nuclear base. Once the USSR acquired the atom bomb, Britain had exposed herself to annihilation without representation. Attlee's government can also be blamed for missing the chance of leading Europe and being in at the start of the Common Market. Others claim that the Labour government had unrealistic expectations of Britain's New Commonwealth, refused to confront the harsh reality of Britain's diminished world status, and (unwisely) retained great power illusions. Some consider that Labour's decision to build an atom bomb was totally misguided.

The debates over the success - or otherwise - of Labour's foreign and imperial policy-making are likely to run and run. There is also another debate. The historian Peter Hennessy has claimed that the period 1948-51 was the last moment when British ministers were in a position to make a decisive contribution as to the direction of British foreign policy and that for the rest of the twentieth century British governments had to live with the consequences of Attlee and Bevin's 'instincts and their analysis, their impulses and their actions'. This is an interesting, but probably too dramatic, claim. It implies that British external policy was henceforth set in concrete - which it was not! It might also seem to imply that Attlee's government had considerable free choice of action - which of course it did not! Like all governments it was constrained by force of circumstance in what it could rationally do. It is probable that had Churchill and the Conservatives been in power in the six years after 1945 British foreign and imperial policy would not have been very different.

Making notes on *'Labour Foreign and Imperial Policy, 1948-51'*

It is worth rereading your notes on the last chapter before commencing making notes on this. Your notes on both chapters should give you an understanding of the main events and decisions taken by Attlee's government between 1945-51, and enable you to assess the statesmanship of the Labour government (especially Ernest Bevin). As you read the chapters try to identify whether Bevin's aims were sound. What could or should he have done that was different? Was Russia as great a threat as Bevin supposed? Was Attlee's government wise to tie Britain so closely to the USA? Could more have been done with the Empire/Commonwealth? Should Labour be blamed for missing the European 'bus'? To what extent did Attlee's government actually achieve its aims?

Answering essay questions on 'Labour Foreign and Imperial Policy, 1948-51'

It is likely you will use information from the last two chapters to answer questions on the success (or otherwise) of British foreign and imperial policy in the period 1945-51. Consider the following questions on Labour foreign policy:

1   'A truly great Foreign Secretary'. Discuss this view of Ernest Bevin.
2   To what extent did the Labour government (1945-51) achieve its aims in foreign and imperial policy?
3   Assess the foreign and imperial policies of Attlee's Labour Government (1945-51).
4   Examine and explain the changes in Britain's relationships with the USA and the USSR between 1945 and 1951.

Re-arrange the questions in order of difficulty. Which do you think is the easiest and which the most difficult? Be prepared to explain why. Many people will identify question 3 as the easiest because, on the surface, it can be answered in a straightforward, descriptive manner. It is because such questions can be answered simply - at a low level - that they are dangerous. It is very easy to write a long, narrative, year-by-year answer but to score only half marks. The key word in the question is 'Assess'. This means you are being asked to make judgements about the successes and the failures of the Labour government. Did the policy-makers achieve their aims? Were these aims sound? Another problem with this question is what to include and what to omit. You will presumably want to have paragraphs on the Russian threat, relations with the USA, imperial policy, and dealings with Western Europe. However, you will not have time to get bogged down in too much detail about such things as the Berlin air-lift or the Korean war. Instead you must be ruthless in summarising the main points so that you can press on to answer the set question.

Question 4 might also cause difficulty. 'Examine and explain' questions often seem easy enough but the difficulty with this question is that students often fail to do what the question says - examine AND explain! It is relatively easy to list the main aspects of Britain's relations with the USA and the USSR. However, to score high marks you do need to explain why British policy-makers acted as they did, stressing that Britain's relationship with the USA was very much determined by both countries fear of the USSR. You will need to examine and explain why, when and how this joint fear developed. Try drawing up a rough plan for this question. What would your introduction be? What paragraphs would you have? What would be your conclusion?

Source-based questions on 'Labour Foreign and Imperial Policy, 1948-51'

1 North Atlantic Defence
Read the Bevin aide-memoire and Article 5 of the North Atlantic Treaty on pages 60, 61 and 63. Answer the following questions.
a)   What did Bevin mean by a 'regional Atlantic Approaches Pact of Mutual Assistance'? (4 marks)
b)   Why did he think there was a need for such a Pact in 1948? (6 marks)
c)   Explain Bevin's comment, 'The alternative is to repeat our experience with Hitler'. (6 marks)
d)   Why might the wording of Article 5 be considered tortuous? (5 marks)

2 Britain and the USA and the USSR
Examine the cartoons on pages 62 and 69. Answer the following questions.
a)   Identify the 3 characters in Vicky's cartoon. (3 marks)
b)   Comment on the sign, 'Seeds of War' in Vicky's cartoon. (4 marks)
c)   What point is Vicky trying to make? (5 marks)
d)   When might Vicky's cartoon have been drawn? (4 marks)
e)   What point is Low trying to make? (4 marks)
f)   Comment on the date of Low's cartoon. (3 marks)
g)   Comment on the differences between the two cartoons. (7 marks)

3 Britain and Europe
Examine the cartoon reproduced on page 62 and read Plowden's account on page 71. Answer the following questions.
a)   Identify the 6 men in the cartoon. (6 marks)
b)   What point is the cartoonist trying to make? (7 marks)
c)   What reasons does Plowden give to justify Britain's response to the Schuman Plan? (7 marks)
d)   Comment on Plowden's last sentence. (5 marks)

CHAPTER 5

Conservative Foreign and Imperial Policy, 1951-5

1 The Situation in 1951

In October 1951 Winston Churchill returned as Prime Minister and Anthony Eden returned as Foreign Secretary. Foreign policy had been an important issue in the general election and it was expected that the new government would assert more authority in world affairs than Attlee's government. This was certainly Churchill and Eden's intention. Both men were convinced that Britain's presence at the 'top table' was essential for the benefit of Britain and the world. The hopes that Britain would remain a great power had some foundation. In 1951 Britain was still the third greatest power in the world - a long way behind the USA and the USSR - but well ahead of all other competitors. In the early 1950s Churchill popularised the idea of 'three great circles' - the Commonwealth, the English-speaking world and Europe. 'If you think of the three inter-linked circles', Churchill argued, 'you will see that we are the only country which has a great part in every one of them'. Britain's influence in each circle was reinforced by its role in the other two. For much of Churchill's premiership it did seem that Britain's unique position enabled her to play a major role in world affairs.

Churchill's aims were clearly stated in a party political broadcast in 1951:

1 At the General Election much party capital was made by calling me 'a warmonger'. That was not true. Now that I am at the head of the Government I shall work ardently in harmony with our allies for peace. If war comes it will be because of world forces beyond
5 Britain's control. On the whole I do not think it will come. Whatever happens we shall stand up with all our strength in defence of the free world against Communist tyranny and aggression. We shall do our utmost to preserve the British Commonwealth and Empire as an independent factor in world
10 affairs. We shall cherish the fraternal association of the English-speaking world. We shall work in true comradeship for and with United Europe.

Stating aims was easy. Achieving them was much harder. It was soon obvious that Churchill and Eden faced exactly the same problems as those which had faced Attlee and Bevan. 'Things have gotten ten or fifteen times more complicated', moaned Churchill. 'The problems I now face are much greater in number and complexity than they used to be'.

In many respects the number one problem facing the Conservative government was the state of the British economy. Although the economy was recovering, Britain faced increasing competition from Germany, France and Japan whose economies were improving far more rapidly than Britain's. Domestic economic crisis, combined with international upheaval, created an atmosphere of gloom in which many problems seemed insoluble. In December 1952 Evelyn Shuckburgh, Eden's private secretary, wrote in his diary:

> 1 Slept badly and became very depressed about the world in general. Our economic situation, German and Japanese competition, destruction of British influence in the Mediterranean and Middle East ... the Americans not backing us anywhere. In fact, having
> 5 destroyed the Dutch empire, the United States are now engaged in undermining the French and British empires as hard as they can.

The Treasury continually warned the government that Britain was carrying too many foreign responsibilities in relation to her resources. Both Churchill and Eden acknowledged that some reappraisal of Britain's foreign and defence policies were necessary. Churchill, however, had no intention of allowing Britain to become a second rate power. Eden perhaps accepted the logic of the Treasury's case more than Churchill. However, he was opposed to Britain quickly jettisoning her overseas commitments, arguing that this would do untold damage to both her international status and to her economy.

2 Churchill and Eden

By 1951 Churchill was far from the towering presence he had been during the Second World War. He was 77, had already suffered two strokes, and was to suffer two more in the course of his premiership. According to his doctor, his old capacity for work had gone and with it much of his self-confidence. Churchill said in 1954, 'I feel like an aeroplane at the end of its flight, in the dusk, with the petrol running out, in search of a safe landing.' Increasingly deaf, he coped with day to day business but perhaps lacked the drive and energy to follow up ideas. Some contemporaries thought he obstructed effective policy-making. In August 1953 Evelyn Shuckburgh noted in his diary:

> 1 All this week we are trying to conduct our foreign policy through the PM who is at Chartwell and always in the bath or asleep or too busy having dinner when we want urgent decisions. He had to be consulted about drafting points in the reply to the Soviets; about
> 5 every individual 'intelligence' operation (which he usually forbids for fear of upsetting the Russians); about telegrams to Persia and

Egypt. We are constantly telephoning minutes and draft telegrams down to Chartwell.

However, Churchill's mental and physical failings can be exaggerated. The Prime Minister still had a fine brain and remained an impressive performer both in Parliament and in Cabinet. Lord Alexander recalled Churchill's method of dealing with his Cabinet:

1 If there was something he wanted done he would set about it very carefully. First he put his proposal, quite simply. Then if he saw frowns around the Cabinet table, he would turn on the charm. 'This', he would say, 'is something very close to my heart. It is my
5 deepest wish. For many years I have believed in it, and now ...'. If, after all that, we were still frowning he would try a tougher line, exerting his power. 'After all, gentlemen, I am Prime Minister ...'. When even this failed to work, and we were obviously going to turn it down, he would say: 'Well, the Cabinet is a place for thrashing
10 out ideas. We mustn't rush into a decision on this. Why don't we go away - and you can think about what I've said. I'm sure, when you've had time to think it over, you will come round to my view'.

Churchill also continued to dominate Parliament: his performances in April 1955 were still 'as brilliant as those of any stage of his career', according to The Scotsman newspaper. The belief that Churchill was 'ga-ga' during his last years can thus be viewed as unfair - or wrong!

Anthony Eden was easily the most important member of Churchill's Cabinet. Most people at the time assumed that Churchill and Eden had virtually identical aims and worked closely together. The truth was not so simple. There was some personal suspicion, if not animosity, between the two men. In 1951 Churchill had intimated that he would hand over the premiership to Eden within a year. To Eden's chagrin, the year became two and then three. Churchill, moreover, had some doubts about whether Eden was really the right man to succeed him. Nor did the two men always see eye to eye on foreign policy. Churchill tended to mistrust the Foreign Office as 'too prone to appease'. He still dreamed of dominating foreign policy, as he had in the Second World War, and whenever Eden was away - even for his honeymoon in 1952 - assumed control of the Foreign Office and launched policy initiatives. This meddling increasingly angered Eden. Nevertheless, the differences between Churchill and Eden should not be exaggerated. To a large extent Churchill relied on Eden's judgement and gave him a remarkably free hand. Virtually everyone, including Churchill, acknowledged that Eden was the Prime Minister-in-waiting.

Eden seemed the 'glamour boy' of British politics, holding an exciting job in which he showed tremendous skill. In reality, both the job and Eden were perhaps less impressive. The Foreign Secretaryship was possibly the most demanding post in the Cabinet. Eden said the job 'had killed Bevin and destroyed Morrison and now he understood why'. After several weeks he admitted that he was 'hardly abreast of the daily telegrams'. Over-worked and unwilling to delegate, he found himself under considerable stress, not eased by constant travelling, and was dogged by ill-health until the end of 1953.

Some historians are critical of Eden, regarding him as an intellectual lightweight, a man who, in Anthony Adamthwaite's view, 'had great flair but no genius' and no 'vision and ability to think ahead'. However, this is perhaps over-harsh. Eden did score some major triumphs in the period 1951-5 and was a first class negotiator. Although there were few major changes in direction after 1951, Eden conducted foreign policy in a manner very different from Morrison. It seemed to many at the time that Britain was again represented with style and assurance abroad.

3 The 'Special Relationship'

Churchill, half-American himself and with a romantic affection for the whole of the 'English-Speaking Peoples', was the leading exponent of the special relationship with the USA. Convinced that partnership with America was vital for Britain's security, and believing (wrongly) that Anglo-American relationships had deteriorated under Attlee, he was determined to work closely with America's leaders, in the same way that he had worked with Roosevelt during the war. Accepting that Britain was now very much a junior partner of the alliance, his main aim was to achieve as full a degree of consultation with the USA as possible, hoping that he might thus restrict the more extreme excesses of American policy and guide it in a direction suitable to British interests.

Churchill and Eden established reasonable relations with Truman and his Secretary of State, Acheson. The British encouraged the Americans to take a more conciliatory approach in the peace discussions with the North Koreans but at the same time supported their firm stand on basic principles. Churchill had no doubts that the USA and Britain had been right to resist North Korean aggression and was prepared to stay in Korea to maintain the moral authority of the United Nations.

The prospect of Anglo-American co-operation seemed to be strengthened when General Dwight D. Eisenhower was elected President in 1952. Churchill and Eisenhower had worked closely together during the Second World War and liked and respected each other. They regularly exchanged letters but met only twice while they were both in office, at Bermuda in 1953 and in Washington in 1954.

However, perhaps the closeness of the special relationship should not be overemphasised. Churchill recognised that Britain and America did not have identical views and interests. The two countries, for example, differed over their approach to the Cold War. In the early 1950s many Americans were obsessed by the communist threat and Joseph Macarthy led the so-called 'witch-hunts' - attempts to root out suspected communists from key positions in the USA. President Eisenhower's Secretary of State, John Foster Dulles, seemed determined to resist communist expansion, possibly even at the risk of war. He even spoke of rolling back the communist 'empire' and liberating Eastern Europe. Churchill, on the other hand, was prepared to take a more conciliatory line, hoping to bring about some kind of detente with Russia.

Eden was even more suspicious of some aspects of American policy than Churchill and believed that Britain could and should take a more independent line to protect her own traditional interests. Anglo-American relations were perhaps not helped by the fact that Eden and Dulles eyed each other with some suspicion - although the animosity between the two men has sometimes been exaggerated. In time Eden realised that American policy in practice was more moderate than Dulles' pronouncements made him fear.

British influence in Washington was significant. Britain remained the USA's main and most powerful ally with a global empire that was increasingly important in the containment of communism. Moreover, many American officials, while having little patience with British pretensions, did respect both Churchill and Eden. Eisenhower's administration was prepared to listen to - if not always take - Britain's advice on major questions.

4 Relations with the USSR

Churchill, somewhat ironically given his long anti-communist stance, came to office committed to improving relations with the USSR if at all possible. Fearing the terrible consequences of a nuclear war and believing that the West was now sufficiently united and well-armed to speak to the USSR from a position of strength, he thought nothing could be lost by talking with the Soviet leaders. The fact that he might be able to carve out a role for himself as a great 'peacemaker' (his reputation as a 'warmonger' was already assured), may also have been a reason why detente with the USSR became one of his major aims.

There was no immediate improvement in east-west relations. The USA, still bearing the brunt of the fighting in Korea, had little interest in talks with Russia. Given that McCarthyism was such a formidable force in America, neither Truman nor Eisenhower wished to be accused of being 'soft' on communism. Most British and French policy makers supported the tough American line.

However, the death of Stalin in March 1953 provided a real opportunity to improve relations with Russia. The new Soviet government seemed more conciliatory. Eden's incapacitation from April to October 1953, following a gall stone operation, enabled Churchill to take over personal control of foreign policy and to pursue his dream of detente. In May he called publicly for an informal summit conference on the lines of Yalta and Potsdam to capitalise on the new mood in Moscow. This declaration attracted support from the Labour opposition and from large sections of the British public. But Churchill had acted without consulting his Cabinet or properly informing the Foreign Office and the USA. Almost immediately opposition to his scheme, both within the Foreign Office and abroad, mounted. Eisenhower, who believed that the new Russian leaders were still committed to the cause of expansion of world communism, urged Churchill to show greater caution. Churchill's stroke in the summer of 1953 prevented further action on his part. However, the end of the Korean war in July 1953 went some way to easing Cold War tension.

In July 1954, again without consulting his Cabinet or the Foreign Office, Churchill sent a cable to the Russians sounding them out on the possibility of a personal visit. This well-meaning action horrified Eden, (he disliked Churchill's meddling and perhaps the fact he was taking centre stage), and resulted in threats of resignation from several Cabinet members. Churchill was unrepentant. However, the Russian government rebuffed the offer - thus preventing a political crisis in Britain! Although continuing to hope that a meeting with the Russian leaders was possible, Churchill's policy during his last six months in office, differed little from that of Eden and the USA: if anything he offended the Soviet leaders more than anyone else during this period. In March 1955 he made a speech to Parliament defending his Russian policy, arguing he had always sought detente with Russia and blaming the failure for this squarely on the Russians. The Soviet response was to blame Britain.

In pursuing his goal of detente with Russia, Churchill demonstrated idealism, determination and cunning. But the complexities of the international scene, divisions within the western alliance and his own health, ensured the failure of his last crusade.

5 China and Indo-China

Britain and the USA found themselves at odds with each other both over their relations with China and with regard to policy in Indo-China. Churchill and Eden, conscious of the limits of British power in the Far East, and fearing full-scale war and the possible loss of Hong Kong, were prepared to seek accommodation with China and, unlike America, were not opposed to the entry of China into the United Nations. US intransigence over non-recognition of China, coupled with the massive support America gave to the Nationalist regime on Taiwan, was viewed in London as a serious hurdle to exploiting differences between China and Russia, and also to easing the Cold War.

Differences between the USA's tough line and the softer British line were apparent in the way both countries responded to the problems of Indo-China, 'the most dangerous and acute of the problems with which I had to deal during my last four years as Foreign Secretary', wrote

Eden. From 1945 France had struggled to maintain some kind of colonial authority in Indo-China. By 1950 French-backed governments in Vietnam, Cambodia and Laos were struggling against communist-led insurgents in North Vietnam who were aided by China. The USA gave the French massive financial assistance. The American government accepted the 'domino' theory and thought that if Vietnam fell, the whole of Indo-China - and possibly the whole of Asia - might follow. The French struggle against communist forces reached its climax in 1954 in the siege of Dien Bien Phu. In Washington there were demands for US air and navy action against the Chinese coastline and/or active intervention in Indo-China itself to assist the French. Eisenhower, however, having just extricated America from Korea, was not keen to plunge his country into another Asian quagmire. Nor was he willing to shoulder responsibility alone. One of Eisenhower's conditions for full US involvement in Vietnam was British support.

Eden, regarding Vietnam as of little importance and fearing that involvement might escalate into a third world war, made it clear that he was not prepared to support US military action. Instead, he favoured a peaceful solution to the problems of Indo-China, and supported the idea of an international conference, which the Russians indicated that they would also support. Differences over policy subjected the Anglo-American relationship to grave strain. However, in February 1954 the USA (albeit reluctantly), China, Russia, France and Britain agreed to meet in Geneva in May 1954.

Just before the meeting, Dien Bien Phu fell to the communists and French rule in Indo-China collapsed. Dulles, still reluctant to be seen making any kind of concession to communism, played little role at Geneva. Eden and Molotov, the Russian Foreign Minister, acted as joint chairmen and enjoyed a surprisingly good working relationship. Eden played a major role in steering the Geneva Conference to what many saw at the time as a successful conclusion.

The Geneva accords signed in July 1954, accepted that Laos and Cambodia should be neutral. Vietnam was to be temporarily partitioned along the 17th parallel pending the holding of free elections in 1956. In the meantime North Vietnam was left under communist control while South Vietnam was to be under the control of a pro-western regime. Partition had long been the preferred British option and the Geneva Conference is still usually seen as a great triumph for Eden. Arguably it prevented another dreadful war in Asia and gave the West breathing space to establish a progressive regime in South Vietnam.

However, Eden's role at Geneva angered many Americans who believed they had lost a good opportunity to smash communism in Indo-China once and for all. The American administration saw Geneva as yet another example of British appeasement and refused to sign the Geneva accords. Although the Geneva Conference might be seen as a success in the short term - for a few years peace was more or less preserved - some would argue that it simply laid the seeds for the Vietnam war of the 1960s and 1970s.

Soon after the Geneva Conference, the South-East Asia Treaty Organisation (SEATO) was formed. At the outset there was considerable argument as to which countries should participate. The eventual founder-members were the USA, Britain, France, Australia, New Zealand, the Philippines, Thailand and Pakistan. This excluded not only both Vietnams, but also Laos, Cambodia and the Chinese Nationalist government on Taiwan. The hope was that this would be an organisation comparable with NATO. However SEATO, unlike NATO, had no standing army or joint command and the member states had much more freedom in determining whether or not to intervene in a crisis. The organisation never realised the expectations of its founders.

6 Defence and Deterrence

By the early 1950s there was increasing concern at the cost of British defence spending. Britain spent more per head on defence than the USA and the Treasury repeatedly called for cuts arguing that defence policies were imposing an excessive burden on the economy. In 1952 the Chiefs of Staff produced a Global Strategy Paper that signalled the way for future defence policy. Arguing that defence expenditure had to be guided by what the economy could afford, the Chiefs of Staff advocated a strategy built around the nuclear deterrent. Nuclear bombs would ensure Britain was adequately defended and should allow a reduction in expenditure on conventional forces.

Until 1952 Britain was totally dependent on the USA for its nuclear deterrent yet had no influence over American use of the bomb. Moreover, the development of US atomic bases in Britain meant, in Churchill's words, that the country had probably become 'the bull's eye of a Soviet attack'. Churchill did his best to revive the wartime nuclear alliance, claiming that America should exchange more information on nuclear matters and that Britain should have some say over the use of the atomic bomb. But the best he could obtain from Truman was a promise that the use of US bases in Britain 'in an emergency would be a matter for joint decision' between the US and British governments, 'in the light of the circumstances prevailing at the time'. Eisenhower, believing that Britain had been unfairly treated, and that closer nuclear co-operation would be of benefit to the USA, was more sympathetic. But opposition in Congress to disclosure of information to Britain remained strong and Eisenhower was only able to secure limited nuclear information-sharing.

Given this impasse, Britain's determination to produce her own nuclear deterrent was understandable. Attlee's government had paved the way and Britain became the third nuclear power in the world, testing its own atomic bomb in October 1952. By then the thermonuclear age was dawning, with American and Russian tests of H-bombs in 1952 and

1953 respectively. Churchill observed 'that we were now as far from the atomic bomb as the atomic bomb itself [was] from the bow and arrow'. In July 1954 the Cabinet decided that Britain must produce her own H-bomb. Although there was - and is - a moral objection to the production of nuclear weapons, Britain's A- and H-bomb decisions showed a strategic rationality. Churchill spoke hopefully of a world actually made safer by the nuclear stalemate. Like Attlee and Bevin, he insisted that 'we could not expect to maintain our influence as a world power unless we possessed the most up-to-date nuclear weapons'. The H-bomb was also seen as a way of ensuring 'more respect for our views' in the USA although how this would happen was unclear.

By the mid-1950s Britain had a stock-pile of atomic bombs, was well on its way to testing its own H-bomb, and had its own nuclear strike force as the long-range V-bombers came into service. But increasing nuclear capacity did not mean it was easy to cut conventional forces. The army pointed out that nuclear weapons offered no solution to the problem of fighting insurgents in overseas territories. The navy argued that conventional fighting would still be necessary, even after the dropping of nuclear bombs. However, after 1951 there were real reductions in defence spending and in the number of British servicemen.

7 Europe

Churchill and Eden faced two main problems in Europe: how far would they support or react towards moves to European unity: and how might they reconcile France to German rearmament. These issues were linked.

a) European Unity

In the late 1940s Churchill had spoken out for European unity. But once in office he was to disappoint the hopes of European federalists. Churchill believed in Europe as a means of bringing France and Germany together, 'for them but not for us'. In November 1951 he told the Cabinet:

> 1 I never thought that Britain or the British Commonwealth should, either individually or collectively, become an integral part of a European federation ... Our first object is the unity and consolidation of the British Commonwealth and what is left of the
> 5 former British Empire. Our second, the 'fraternal association' of the English-speaking world; and third, United Europe, to which we are a separate, closely- and specially-related ally and friend.

Eden felt similarly. He told an American audience that the British people knew in their bones that they could not join a European federation.

However many Europeans, with American support, were determined to promote the integration of Western Europe. In 1951 the European Coal and Steel Community (ECSC) had been set up, its aim to provide for the free movement of coal and steel throughout the six member countries. Such was the success of the ECSC that a special conference of Foreign Ministers of the Six (Germany, France, Italy, Holland, Belgium and Luxemburg) was held at Messina in 1955 to see what further steps might be taken. Britain viewed these developments with some concern - but hoped that disagreements between the various countries would prevent further moves towards European unity.

b) European Defence and German Rearmament

By 1951 there were growing moves towards European unity in defence as well as in economic matters. However, the prospect of a joint European army arose more from French fears of a rearmed Germany than any great federalist desire for unity. Since 1950 America had pressed strongly for German rearmament as the best way to ensure NATO forces stood some chance of combating Russian forces. In order to prevent the growth of an independent German army, the French proposed setting up a European Defence Community (EDC). This would consist of a European army under a European Ministry of Defence. European forces would be closely integrated and there would be a common budget paid for by European taxes. This plan was finally thrashed out and signed (but not ratified) by France, Germany, Italy and the Benelux countries in 1952.

The USA accepted the EDC plan but Churchill was less than enthusiastic. He had no wish to be drawn into a European federation and regarded the EDC idea as military nonsense - a 'sludgy amalgam'. He would have preferred to see Germany directly rearmed within NATO. Under considerable American pressure, he finally agreed in principle to the EDC but refused to allow Britain to become a member. The most he would do was accept that Britain would establish close 'association' with the EDC. The EDC continued to be the subject of lengthy negotiations as France, in particular, strove to extract more precise British military commitments. Eden was unenthusiastic about keeping a fixed number of British troops in Europe which might be seen as the first step on the slippery slope to joining a European federation. But in order to appease the French and Americans, Britain finally did agree to put forces at the EDC's disposal.

However, in August 1954 four years of intense negotiations came to nothing when the whole EDC project was rejected by the French National Assembly. The NATO alliance was thrown into confusion. Dulles had already warned of an 'agonizing reappraisal' of US policy towards Europe if the EDC collapsed. Fears of an American relapse into isolationism seemed to require a decisive British response. The main problem was how to persuade France to agree to German rearmament. Eden now pulled off a diplomatic triumph. Shuttling between European capitals in September 1954 he proposed that West Germany should be admitted into NATO on equal terms, except that it should renounce the right to the so-called ABC weapons - atomic, bacteriological and chemical. The stumbling block was France. What finally decided matters for the French was Eden's readiness to make a further concession and agree to a permanent British troop commitment. At a nine power Conference in London in September Britain undertook to keep the existing four British divisions and tactical air force then assigned to NATO forces in Germany and not to withdraw them unilaterally unless there was a grave overseas or financial crisis. The agreements - or accords - signed on this basis in Paris in October 1954 satisfied the French Assembly. In May 1955 West Germany was first recognised as a sovereign state, then entered NATO and the process of West German rearmament began.

Russia denounced the Paris accords and set up the Warsaw Pact in retaliation. Given the Russian dominance of Eastern Europe this was hardly a major diplomatic or military blow. West German rearmament, on the other hand, greatly strengthened the West. Although Churchill was not particularly impressed by Eden's work, others thought that his diplomatic skill had saved the Atlantic alliance.

8 The Middle East

Churchill and Eden were determined to maintain Britain's premier position in the Middle East. The defence of Britain's interests depended partly upon Britain's own military strength in the area but also on working partnerships with a number of powers, particularly Iraq and Jordan. As long as these states were closely aligned with her, Britain could overawe other Arab states. The USA, with a host of commitments elsewhere, was happy to give Britain a reasonably free hand, provided Russia was kept out of the region. However, Britain's main problems in the early 1950s came more from Iran and Egypt than from Russia.

a) Iran

Churchill's government inherited the problem of Iran. The loss of Iranian oil in 1951 had been both a serious financial blow and a blow to British prestige. However, despite Labour fears, Churchill's government did not rush into military action in 1951-2, preferring instead to see how matters developed. The great international oil companies stuck together and refused to handle Iranian oil. In consequence Iranian oil production plummeted and the Iranian people were soon suffering great hardships. Eden was confident that the radical leader Mussadiq would fall and be succeeded by a more 'reasonable' government. The USA, fearing that

Mussadiq might well come under communist influence finally decided to support Britain and work for his downfall. In August 1953 American and British intelligence helped engineer a coup which led to the overthrow of Mussadiq. The new Iranian government quickly negotiated an oil agreement with Britain. The Anglo-Iranian Oil Company - now called British Petroleum - received compensation for its losses and in future oil profits were to be shared between the Iranian Government and an international consortium. It seemed that the humiliation of 1951 had been avenged and that Britain had enjoyed a great success. But that success had only been achieved with US help, and concessions made to American oil companies angered many British politicians and businessmen. After 1953 Britain's position in the world oil market declined and the Americans played a more important role in Middle Eastern oil politics.

b) Egypt

Pre-1951 the British and Egyptian governments had been unable to reach agreement over the Suez Canal Zone or over who should be responsible for the Sudan. Churchill regarded the Suez base as of vital importance to Britain, a connecting link on a strategic chain stretching to Singapore and the Far East. However, the Anglo-Egyptian Treaty of 1936 was due to expire in 1956. Thereafter Britain could not lawfully maintain troops in any part of Egypt without the assent of the Egyptian government: assent which would certainly not be given.

At the start of 1952 Anglo-Egyptian relations, bad at the best of times, deteriorated further. Egyptian nationalist fervour increased and British forces were subject to sabotage and attack by Egyptian guerillas. Riots occurred in Cairo and large numbers of business premises were destroyed. Churchill was confident that the 80,000 British troops in the Canal Zone could hold the military situation. But Britain could not control the political situation. In 1952 a group of young army officers seized power in Egypt and King Farouk was forced into exile (taking with him his remarkable collection of pornographic clocks!).

Discussions on the Sudan and the Canal Zone continued. Somewhat surprisingly, given the ardently nationalist nature of the new regime, there seemed to be a more conciliatory atmosphere. In 1953, despite protests from many Conservative backbench MPs, Britain and Egypt finally reached agreement on the Sudan. The country would have a three year period of virtual home rule. Thereafter it would be free to choose between complete independence or union with Egypt. Britain and Egypt did all they could to influence the elections of a Sudanese Constituent Assembly in whose hands the eventual decision would lie. The Sudanese, to Britain's satisfaction, finally decided in favour of complete independence commencing in 1956.

The Suez Canal proved more difficult. Britain suggested numerous compromises but, since all involved British troops remaining in the Canal Zone, all were rejected by the Egyptians. In 1953 Eden, aware of the danger of worsening relations with Egypt, determined to change tack. He was helped by the fact that the Chiefs of Staff now agreed that the Suez base was no longer essential. Churchill initially fought tooth and nail to stay in Egypt, regarding Eden's new policy as one of 'scuttle'. However, his growing conviction that the thermonuclear age had made large permanent bases vulnerable and obsolete, finally helped reconcile him to the loss of Suez.

Eventually in July 1954 agreement was reached. British troops would be withdrawn from the Canal Zone within 20 months. In the meantime certain key installations would be jointly maintained by British and Egyptian technicians. In the event of an attack upon Egypt, Britain could re-occupy the base. Eden's conciliatory diplomacy seemed to have at last resolved the differences between Egypt and Britain.

Almost immediately, however, the Suez agreement ran into serious trouble. The Conservative backbench rebellion, which had arisen at the time of the Sudan agreement, re-emerged. The so-called 'Suez Group' regarded the abandonment of the Canal as evidence of the loss of will in Britain to maintain its rule in the Middle East - and beyond. Some 40 Conservative MPs intimated that they would vote against any treaty involving withdrawal of troops from Suez. There seemed a real possibility that the government would be defeated. However, the Labour opposition decided to abstain on the critical vote, and the Conservative 'revolt' of 26 MPs was less than had been feared.

Eden believed that the Suez agreement strengthened Britain's position in the Middle East. Britain already exerted considerable influence over Iraq and Jordan and there now seemed a real possibility of drawing Egypt into Britain's 'orbit'. However, in November 1954 Gamal Nasser, a nationalist army officer who was determined to throw off all vestiges of British imperialism, won power in Egypt. This boded ill for future Anglo-Egyptian relations.

c) Cyprus

Churchill and Eden hoped that Cyprus (British since 1878) would become a suitable alternative base from which Britain could sustain her dominance in the Middle East. However, by 1954 it was evident that most Greek Cypriots (80 per cent of the island's population) wanted union with Greece, a move strongly opposed by the Turkish minority. The Foreign Office made it clear that the island was to remain permanently British. The Greek Cypriots, led by Archbishop Makarios, pressed their demands and a guerilla organisation (called Eoka) waged a terrorist campaign against Britain. Britain declared a state of emergency and sent 25,000 troops to maintain law and order.

10 Imperial Concerns

In 1951 the Empire/Commonwealth remained vital to Britain's economic interests, supplying 49 per cent of Britain's imports and taking 54 per cent of Britain's exports. The Empire/Commonwealth was also vital if Britain was to remain a great world power. In the early 1950s Commonwealth Conferences, chaired by Churchill, continued to be dominated by Britain, and although relations with the old 'white' dominions were not as close as they once had been, the hope remained that the Commonwealth could still become a great force for peace and progress. Churchill had no intention of adopting a policy of full-scale decolonisation and believed it would take many decades before most colonies were ready for independence. In 1951 there was relatively little pressure to force Britain to jettison her remaining colonies. The British public, despite the burden of imperial defence, showed no wish to abandon empire. Nor was there much threat from nationalist movements. In many colonies the population seemed too small to permit easy development towards independence. Federation was a possibility but often the proposed units of a federation (eg in the West Indies) were hundreds of miles apart and had little in common. Elsewhere, as in large parts of Africa, the proportion of educated people seemed too low to permit independence. Within several territories, there was also a problem of ethnic or tribal division, which could easily lead to bloodshed if Britain pulled out too quickly. Throughout the early 1950s British forces continued to fight in Malaya against communist insurgents but with the support of most of the Malayan people.

What is striking about Britain's relations with her colonies in the early 1950s is the wide variation in British attitudes and policy between one region and another. This is particularly apparent in Africa.

a) West Africa

Nigeria and the Gold Coast (Ghana) were two of Britain's most valuable colonies. Both were large, well-populated countries with rising standards of literacy and educated elites capable of taking on the responsibility of government. In neither country were matters complicated by large numbers of white settlers. By 1955 Churchill's Cabinet had accepted that both countries should soon be independent. Most experts thought that independence for Ghana and Nigeria would make little difference to Britain's economic or strategic interests. Therefore the opportunity to adopt a policy of divide and rule - a real possibility given the various ethnic minority groups (especially in Nigeria) - was ignored.

b) East Africa

In Tanganyika, Uganda and Kenya there were few educated Africans, serious tribal divisions, and quite large numbers of Asians, brought into the area by Britain earlier in the century. In Kenya there were also thousands of white settlers, long accustomed to holding local political power as well as social and economic privilege and determined to resist native African rule. The whites knew they had support of many British Conservatives who hoped that Kenya would remain a 'white man's country'.

In East Africa Britain's main plan was to create an East African Federation. The hope was that the black elites in Tanganyika (where there was one European for every 430 Africans) and Uganda (where there were even fewer whites) would be harnessed to a theoretically 'multi-racial' but essentially white-led Kenya. This plan, not surprisingly, encountered black African opposition.

Black Kenyans were particularly unhappy. The Kikuyu tribe, the largest in Kenya, protested against rising prices, the fact that whites held the best land, and other aspects of racial discrimination. The failure of peaceful protest led to violence. From 1952 to 1956 what became known as the Mau Mau emergency took place. Ninety-five Europeans and about 13,000 blacks were killed. Only after the British had sent thousands of troops to Kenya was the Mau Mau rebellion suppressed.

c) Central Africa

In Central Africa, especially in Southern Rhodesia, there were large numbers of white settlers, who already had a great deal of local autonomy and who, like the Kenyan whites, believed they represented a superior civilisation. They had no intention of sacrificing power to the black majority. Plans for establishing a Central African Federation from Northern and Southern Rhodesia and Nyasaland had been drawn up by Attlee's government. Churchill supported this idea and in 1953 the Federation was brought into existence. The Federation's constitution, which talked of 'partnership' between the races, in reality left power in the hands of the whites and was, in consequence, opposed by the black majority. Most black Africans had little faith in British promises of gradual self-rule. Many Rhodesian whites were also disappointed by the fact that Britain did not offer full independence to the new Federation.

11 The End of Churchill

In April 1955 the 80-year-old Sir Winston Churchill at last decided to resign and Sir Anthony Eden became Prime Minister. Historians still debate the success or otherwise of Churchill's peacetime administration. The historian Anthony Adamthwaite has generally been critical, seeing

Churchill and Eden as less successful than Attlee and Bevin. He has criticised them for missing the opportunity of commencing a gradual retreat in world affairs. He has seen Churchill as lacking in drive and energy and has claimed that he had exaggerated ideas about Britain's position in the world, ideas in excess of her military and financial strength. Adamthwaite has also been critical of Eden, who (he has

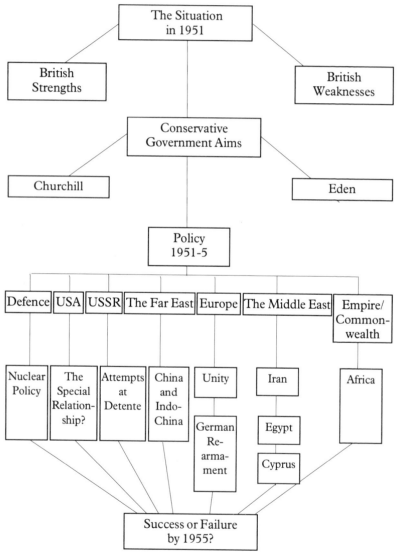

Summary - Conservative Foreign and Imperial Policy, 1951-5

argued) realised the need for reduced commitment, but then did nothing to bring it about. He has claimed that policy-making suffered because Churchill and Eden were frequently at odds. He has blamed Churchill for failing to reform the government policy-making machinery which he has seen as 'more a collection of warring baronies than a single force'. He has also blamed Churchill's administration for missing a number of important opportunities, not least in failing to explore closer economic links with Europe.

However, the historian Anthony Seldon has a more positive view. He has claimed that neither Churchill nor Eden did over-estimate Britain's potential strength. He has argued that there was remarkably little 'gunboat diplomacy'. Churchill's government, for example, did not attack Iran in 1951 and was adamantly opposed to sending forces to Indo-China in 1954. Far from trying to cling on to empire, Britain withdrew from Sudan and Suez and accepted moves towards independence in Ghana and Nigeria. Churchill's government actually reduced defence expenditure. All this does not suggest that Churchill and Eden had unrealistic grand illusions. Arguably both men pursued pragmatic policies and the continuity in colonial, foreign and defence policies between Attlee's and Churchill's governments is striking.

Although Churchill may not have been the force he once had been, he could still display remarkable vision (as in his efforts to build bridges with Russia) and his wartime reputation still carried great weight, both at home and abroad. Seldon has argued that, far from being physically or mentally unfit for the job, Churchill 'has some claim to be regarded as the most considerable British Prime Minister since the war'. He provided a lead and sense of purpose - and then delegated well, standing back and letting others, like Eden, handle the actual detail. Certainly Churchill and Eden could claim some important diplomatic triumphs, not least in 1954 with the Geneva Conference, and the settlement of German rearmament. The situation in 1955 seemed, in many respects, more promising than the situation in 1951. The fact that Britain had a more secure position in the world was, according to Seldon, 'in no small part due to the efforts of the Churchill Government'.

Making notes on *'Conservative Foreign and Imperial Policy, 1951-5'*

When making notes on this chapter you should have one major question in mind: how successful was Churchill's Conservative Government? To help you make your judgement, you might be well advised to organise your notes as follows:
1   What were Churchill (and Eden's) main aims?
2   Were these aims reasonable?
3   What were Britain's strengths and weaknesses in 1951 and beyond?
4   What policies did Britain pursue with regard to:

a) the USA
b) the USSR
c) Indo-China
d) Europe
e) the Middle East
f) the Empire/Commonwealth.
5 How successful was Churchill's second administration?

Answering essay questions on *'Conservative Foreign and Imperial Policy, 1951-5'*

The following are likely questions on this period:
1 How successful was Winston Churchill's second administration (1951-5) in foreign and imperial affairs?
2 'An old man, long past his prime, who was not really in control of events'. Does Churchill's role in foreign and imperial matters 1951-5 bear out this assessment?
3 Assess critically the role of Anthony Eden as Foreign Secretary from 1951-5.

While much of the content of these essays is likely to be similar, the emphasis should be very different. Question 1 is a general question for which this chapter, in particular the 'Making notes' section, should prepare you well! Question 2 asks you to focus on Churchill. Was he a spent force? Were his diplomatic successes more Eden's work than his own? Did Churchill or his government achieve any success in foreign or imperial affairs? It doesn't really matter whether you defend or criticise Churchill, providing you have good evidence at your disposal to argue your case. Remember that examiners are often very impressed by candidates who can present an effective argument that throws doubt on an assumption made in the phrasing of a question.

Question 3 asks you to focus on Anthony Eden. A vital part of preparing to tackle an essay question based on an assessment of anything - or anyone - is consciously to identify the criteria you will use in making your judgement. It is best to state these explicitly in your essay. What criteria would you employ in assessing Eden? You will also need to consider the extent to which Eden had a free hand. Did he merely execute policy determined by Churchill or was he a free agent? Did the two men have similar views? To what extent did they differ? Draw up a rough plan for question 3. What would you be saying in your introduction? How many paragraphs do you envisage writing (7 or 8 is usually about right) and what would be the emphasis of each paragraph? Write down your actual conclusion - and remember to answer the question. Assess Eden's work! What were his successes? What were his failures? Did his successes outweigh his failures?

Source-based questions on 'Conservative Foreign Policy, 1951-5'

1 Churchill's Aims in 1951
Read Churchill's party political broadcast on page 83 and his speech to the Cabinet in November 1951 on page 91. Answer the following questions:
a) Why might Churchill have been called a 'warmonger' in the 1951 General Election? (2 marks)
b) Who would Churchill have seen as Britain's main 'allies for peace'? (2 marks)
c) Why was Churchill opposed to Britain becoming an 'integral part of a European federation'? (2 marks)
d) What did Churchill mean when he spoke of 'the fraternal association of the English-speaking world'? (3 marks)
e) Would you see the two speeches as consistent or inconsistent - and why? (4 marks)
f) What might have been the Labour Party's response to the party political broadcast in 1951? (6 marks)
g) Which of Churchill's aims had been i) achieved, and ii) not achieved by 1955? (6 marks)

2 Britain's Problems in 1952
Read the account of Evelyn Shuckburgh in December 1952 on page 84. Answer the following questions:
a) What is meant by 'German and Japanese competition'? (2 marks)
b) How exactly did Britain exert influence in the Mediterranean and the Middle East? (4 marks)
c) Why was Shuckburgh wary of the USA - and did he have good cause? (4 marks)
d) What are the strengths and weaknesses of this source for historians examining the state of affairs in December 1952? (5 marks)
e) What other sources might a historian need to consult to obtain a more rounded perspective? (5 marks)

3 The Leadership of Winston Churchill
Read the extract from Evelyn Shuckburgh's diary and Lord Alexander's view of Churchill on pages 84 and 85. Answer the following questions:
a) What impression of Churchill do you get from Shuckburgh's account? (5 marks)
b) Why might it be unfair to judge Churchill's conduct of affairs from his actions in August 1953? (5 marks)
c) What impression of Churchill do you get from Lord Alexander's account? (5 marks)
d) What other sources might provide useful evidence about Churchill's mental and physical powers in the early 1950s? (5 marks)

CHAPTER 6

Anthony Eden and Suez, 1955-6

1 Sir Anthony Eden

Few British Prime Ministers have entered office as popular or with such a great reputation as an international statesman as Anthony Eden. An MP since 1923, he had held the post of Foreign Secretary for three periods totalling over ten years (1935-8, 1940-5, 1951-5). In his late 50s, he was a man of charm, intelligence, industry and good looks, a humane and progressive Conservative, respected by many on both left and right for his diplomatic achievements. He seemed a fitting successor to Churchill. Almost immediately, and to prove his popularity, the new Prime Minister called a general election, winning an over-all majority of nearly 60 seats. Eden's position seemed strong. The new Labour Party leader, Hugh Gaitskell, was well to the 'right' within his party and was prepared to support many of Eden's policies. Thus Britain seemed to enjoy unusual 'national unity'.

However, the new leader was far from being 'superman'. Although he had many fine qualities, there were character flaws. He could be bad-tempered, petulant and petty. He was certainly a workaholic, finding it hard to delegate, and tending to live on his nerves. There were other problems. He had few close political friends, even in his own party and had little experience in party management and domestic issues. His tendency to interfere in all aspects of government alienated many of his colleagues and simply increased Eden's work-load.

Given his background, it was not surprising that Eden, like Churchill, gave precedence to foreign rather than to domestic affairs. His first Foreign Secretary, Harold Macmillan, was soon replaced by Selwyn Lloyd. The appointment of Lloyd, a lawyer with limited experience in diplomacy, was a clear sign that Eden intended to control foreign policy personally. His successes over Indo-China and German rearmament in 1954 had left him confident that he could still shape international affairs.

Although Eden had quarrelled with Churchill at various times, his aims were, on the surface, not dissimilar to his former leader's. While accepting that Britain was probably attempting too much in too many areas, he was determined to maintain Britain's influence in the world. His travels had confirmed his sense of the unity of the Commonwealth and he believed that this was the essential foundation of Britain's world power. Like Churchill, he hoped to ease the Cold War which might enable his government to reduce Britain's military commitments, especially in Europe.

However, there were also some important differences between Eden and Churchill. Churchill's belief in co-operation with the USA had been an article of faith. Eden, while accepting the importance of working with the Americans, was far more dubious about their wisdom and integrity. Moreover he showed a greater confidence than Churchill in Britain's ability to function as a great power, if necessary, independently of the USA, especially in the Middle East. In October 1955 Eden told his Cabinet:

> 1 Our interests in the Middle East were greater than those of the United States because of our dependence on Middle East oil, and our experience in the area was greater than theirs. We should not therefore allow ourselves to be restricted overmuch by reluctance
> 5 to act without full American concurrence and support. We should frame our own policy in the light of our interests in the area and get the Americans to support it to the extent we could induce them to do so.

2 The Geneva Summit

By 1955 West German rearmament had finally been achieved and the West felt in a stronger position to meet Russia. In July 1955, therefore, a great power summit, the first meeting of Soviet and Western leaders since 1945, took place at Geneva. The main purpose was to discuss, and if possible resolve, the future of Germany. Not much was achieved. Russia insisted that a reunited Germany should not be allowed to remain in NATO while the Western powers insisted that she should be. Although no specific agreement was reached at the summit, at least no ill will was created and the general atmosphere was reasonably friendly. From Eden's point of view the one really positive outcome of the Conference was the acceptance by the new Soviet leaders, Khrushchev and Bulganin, of an invitation to visit Britain. They came in April 1956 and the fact that they did so seemed to indicate some improvement in East-West relations. However, Khrushchev's blustering behaviour and tendency to threaten seemed likely to cause problems in the future.

3 Europe

In 1955 Britain was invited to join discussions in Brussels on further European integration. Eden was opposed to any idea of European federation but Macmillan argued that Britain could exert a greater influence on the talks if she were a full participant and not just an observer. In the event Britain was represented but only by an official from the Board of Trade. While the Brussels talks progressed, senior British officials examined the issues in detail. Emphasising the importance of Britain's extra-European economic interests, they concluded that British should not commit herself to Europe, that the establishment of a Common Market would, 'on the whole', be bad for

Britain, and that consequently Britain should work to frustrate it. These conclusions were endorsed by the Cabinet without much discussion. European integration still did not seem particularly important.

4 Problems in the Middle East in 1955-6

Eden, aware of the importance of Britain's oil investments, was determined to maintain Britain's dominant position in the Middle East. That position seemed reasonably strong in 1955. Differences with Egypt seemed to have been settled in 1954. Turkey was linked to the West through NATO and Pakistan through SEATO. Iraq and Jordan had staunchly pro-British regimes and Britain continued to have considerable influence in Libya and parts of the Arabian peninsula. Throughout 1955 British and American diplomats worked hard, but ultimately unsuccessfully, to bring about a final settlement of the Arab-Israeli conflict. But Britain was successful in forming a regional security organisation in the Middle East. In February 1955 Turkey and Iraq (with British backing) concluded a military alliance known as the Baghdad Pact. Britain formally joined the Pact in April 1955 and was soon followed by Pakistan and Iran.

The Baghdad Pact was designed largely to contain Soviet influence. However, the main effect of the Pact was to antagonise the Egyptian leader Nasser. Nasser's precise goals are still a matter of debate. But what is certain is that he was opposed to Western (and particularly British) influence in the Middle East. 'Pan-Arabism' - the idea that all Arabic-speaking peoples had an essential identity of interest - had been a growing force for years, and Nasser envisaged himself as the leader of the Arab world. As a result, he bitterly opposed the British-dominated Baghdad Pact, regarding it as a challenge to his authority. He had not been mollified by British concessions to Egypt in 1954 and possibly regarded them as evidence of weakening British resolve. Determined to bring about a reduction of British influence, Nasser encouraged Arab nationalist movements throughout the Middle East. Eden feared that the governments of Jordan and Iraq might either turn against Britain or be replaced by extreme nationalist elements who would certainly do so.

A further cause for concern was that Nasser was not prepared to take the Western side in the Cold War. In September 1955, when the West refused to increase arms supplies to Egypt, he began to purchase weapons from Czechoslovakia. Hitherto Britain, France and the USA had exercised a monopoly of arms supplies to Israel and the Middle East and this had enabled them to regulate the supply. The Egyptian move was thus seen as a threat to the stability of the region. British fears increased when intelligence reports, supposedly from a highly reliable source in Nasser's entourage, stressed that the Egyptian leader was prepared to become a Soviet instrument.

However Eden still hoped that with careful handling Nasser might remain friendly, and arrangements for the evacuation of the last British troops from the Canal Zone proceeded according to plan. In December 1955 Britain, along with the USA and the World bank, agreed to give Egypt financial aid to enable her to build the Aswan Dam, a massive engineering project which would provide Egypt with water from the River Nile. This loan was intended to ensure that Nasser remained within the Western orbit.

But by early 1956 events seemed to indicate that Nasser could not be 'bought'. In March 1956 King Hussain of Jordan dismissed Sir John Glubb, the British soldier who had long commanded the Arab legion, a force largely officered and financed by Britain. Eden blamed Nasser for this move which was undoubtedly a blow to British prestige. To give Nasser vast loans looked like rewarding an enemy at the expense of friends. America, aware that Nasser was flirting with Russia and China, agreed. On 19 July 1956 the British and American loan offer for financing the Aswan Dam was withdrawn.

5 The Nationalisation of the Suez Canal

At a great mass demonstration on 26 July Nasser delivered his reply to the West. To obtain funds for building the Aswan Dam, Egypt would nationalise the Suez Canal Company in which the British government and British and French financial interests had a major stake. Investors would receive the market value of their shares but henceforward the Company would belong entirely to Egypt.

Some legal experts thought that Nasser's action was contrary to international law. But others argued that the Company was legally Egyptian and that Nasser had acted fairly in promising to pay compensation to the shareholders. Only if Nasser, either through inability or malice, failed to keep the Canal open to shipping would Egypt be definitely in breach of international law. Throughout the next few months Nasser took great pains to ensure the Canal remained open.

However, the legalistic arguments were somewhat academic. A vast amount of British trade, especially oil, was dependent on the Canal. Therefore the seizure of the Canal provided Nasser with a future opportunity to blackmail Britain and the West. Moreover, there were issues latent in the dispute which ranked higher than the fate of the Canal. Nasser had clearly thrown down a challenge to Britain and the world order. If he was allowed to get away with his action, his standing throughout the Arab world would be boosted and British prestige would plummet.

Eden determined Nasser must be stopped before he went any further in undermining Britain's position in Middle East. On 27 July he told his Cabinet:

1 The nationalisation [of the Suez Canal] is not just a legal matter, it
is one of the widest international importance ... Colonel Nasser's
action has presented us with an opportunity to find a lasting
settlement of this problem, and we should not hesitate to take
5 advantage of it ... Our essential interests in this area must, if
necessary, be safeguarded by military action and the necessary
preparations to this end must be made ... Even if we have to act
alone, we cannot stop short of using force to protect our position if
all other means of protecting it prove unsuccessful ... Any failure
10 on the part of the Western Powers to take the necessary steps to
regain control over the Canal would have disastrous consequences
for the economic life of the Western Powers and for their influence
in the Middle East.

Kirkpatrick, the Permanent Under-Secretary at the Foreign Office, held
similar views:

1 If we sit back while Nasser consolidates his position and gradually
acquires control of the oil-bearing countries, he can and is,
according to our information, resolved to wreck us ... I doubt
whether we shall be able to pay for the bare minimum necessary for
5 our defence. And a country that cannot provide for its defence is
finished.

Alan Lennox-Boyd, the Colonial Secretary wrote to Eden in August
1956:

I remain firmly convinced that if Nasser wins or even appears to
win we might as well as a government (and indeed as a country) go
out of business.

Eden's determination to destroy Nasser was bouyed-up by such views.
Like many of his advisers, he visualised Nasser as a latter-day Mussolini
(if not quite a Hitler) who must be stopped sooner rather than later. This
view was, perhaps, over-simplistic, but there was some justification for
it. Nasser's regime was developing familiar attributes of a totalitarian
state: suppression of civil liberties; nationalistic, rabble-rousing rhetoric;
organised subversion in other countries; and plans to extend territorial
domination. Eden was not alone in wanting to bring about Nasser's
downfall. Churchill's view was, 'We can't have this malicious swine
sitting across our communications'. The Labour leader Gaitskell
condemned Nasser and a House of Commons debate on 2 August left
the impression of a virtual consensus behind firm action.
    An Egyptian Committee of the Cabinet, initially consisting of Eden,
Selwyn Lloyd, Harold Macmillan, Lord Salisbury, Alec Douglas Home
and Sir Walter Monckton, was set up to supervise the day-to-day

conduct of the crisis. It seems clear that other members of the Cabinet were kept well-informed by Eden and that the broad lines of his strategy received full Cabinet approval.

6 British Policy, July-October 1956

With hindsight, Eden's best course of action might have been to send forces immediately against Nasser. This was the advice of the Iraqi leader Nuri Said, who urged Britain to 'hit Nasser hard and quickly'. Eden knew that he could count on French support. The French, who also had a financial stake in the Suez Canal Company, held Nasser responsible for much of the trouble they were encountering in Algeria and saw the Suez crisis as a means of stopping him radiating his dangerous appeal across the Arab world. French leaders were quite prepared to use force.

However immediate action was ruled out by two factors. First Eden was told by the combined Chiefs of Staff that military action would take at least six weeks to prepare. Secondly President Eisenhower made it clear that he was strongly opposed to the use of force. The American President, while agreeing that Nasser was a threat to Western interests, preferred more covert operations to overthrow him. The threat to the Suez Canal did not greatly effect American interests and the American government was reluctant to be associated with anything that smacked of colonialism and which might rebound to the benefit of communism. The American view was that the crisis might well be solved by negotiation and that this was not the issue upon which to try to topple Nasser. Eisenhower, standing for re-election in November, had no wish to be involved in a military adventure which might threaten his chances of a second term in office. American support was vital because, in the event of a crisis, Britain would be dependent on American oil and financial backing.

Eden, therefore, determined to make a virtue of necessity and agreed to negotiate for the time being. Meanwhile Britain and France applied all possible pressure, short of war, against Egypt. Britain's stated objective was not to restore the Suez Canal Company but instead to put the Canal under some sort of international control. Eden's private aim, however, remained the toppling of Nasser, whether by force or as a result of a diplomatic defeat, which would so damage his prestige that he might well fall. Plans for an assault on Egypt (code-named Operation Musketeer) and the build up of British forces in the East Mediterranean continued. By early September the Chiefs of Staff supported an attack on Port Said, rather than on Alexandria, on the grounds that this was likely to result in lower civilian casualties and fit the pretext that Britain was simply trying to recover her property.

In mid-August a conference of nations most dependent on the Canal was convened in London. The vast majority supported an American proposal that Egyptian sovereignty over the Canal should be recognised but that the Canal should be run by an international body, which would include Egypt. Nasser rejected these proposals outright. At a second conference in September, a more detailed American plan for a Suez Canal Users Association was agreed. But this plan made little sense unless it was backed by force and the American Secretary of State Dulles made it clear that the USA had no intention of using force. Lacking 'teeth', as Dulles himself admitted, the Users Association achieved nothing.

The USA and the Labour Party hoped that a negotiated settlement could be worked out in the United Nations. In October Britain put forward a number of resolutions but the Security Council failed to reach unanimous agreement, the USSR and Yugoslavia effectively vetoing the British proposals. Nasser was not prepared to come forward with specific Egyptian proposals and UN negotiations quickly floundered.

Unfortunately the longer negotiations continued the less easy it became to justify military action. The USA still refused to support or condone armed intervention. By now the Labour Party had also made it clear that it would only support British action which had the consent of the United Nations, which as both Eden and the Labour leadership knew, would never be forthcoming. Some Conservative MPs wanted re-assurance that all practicable steps had been taken to ensure a settlement by peaceful means before they would back the use of force. Even some of Eden's Cabinet were hesitant and Monckton, the Minister of Defence, was opposed to some of the proposed military measures.

By October it was clear to Eden that negotiations were getting nowhere. Aware that many members of his own party were pressing for strong action and that the large force concentrating in the East Mediterranean could not be allowed to remain idle indefinitely, Eden was anxious to force the issue as soon as possible. However, if Britain was to attack Egypt an excuse for action, acceptable to both British and world opinion, was seen as essential.

7 The Sèvres Plan

Israel, like Britain and France, was alarmed by Nasser's action, by his growing prestige and by the fact that he portrayed himself as the Arab champion who would lead them to victory against Israel. He ensured that Israeli ships were banned from the Suez Canal and Egyptian commandos mounted attacks on Israel from bases in Sinai. Israel was determined to take retaliatory action and display her own strength to Egypt and the rest of the Arab world. However, the Israeli government wanted Britain as a military ally before mounting an operation against Egypt. Until October 1956 British-Israeli co-operation seemed unlikely because Britain had tended to favour the Arab, rather than the Jewish, cause.

France and Israel, on the other hand, had had close links for some time and in September the two countries had secret talks in which a joint attack on Egypt was considered. Both countries were prepared to take action with or without American approval but both regarded British assistance as vital. The idea of co-operation between Britain, France and Israel seems to have first been put to Eden on 14 October. The French proposed that Israeli forces should attack Egypt across the Sinai. Britain and France, having given Israeli troops enough time to seize most of the Sinai, would then order both sides to withdraw their forces from the Suez Canal. This would allow an Anglo-French force to intervene and occupy the Canal on the pretext of saving it from damage by the fighting. Britain and France would thus be able to claim to be acting as peacemakers while actually seizing control of the Canal.

Eden, realising that this plan would provide a new excuse to justify military intervention, was enthusiastic. On 16 October he and Foreign Secretary Selwyn Lloyd had a top-secret meeting in Paris and underwrote the French scheme. Two days later the Cabinet was informed - or partly informed - about the plan and approved it. On 22 October Selwyn Lloyd secretly met the Israeli Prime Minister and leading French politicians in Paris, reporting back to his British colleagues the next day. By 24 October plans had been worked out in considerable detail and agreement finally reached between Britain, France and Israel. The following extract, from the Protocol of Sèvres, is believed to be an accurate English translation of the original French. The official English copies of the Protocol have never come to light. (Eden attempted to have all evidence of the conspiracy destroyed and denied all knowledge of collusion in Parliament and in his memoirs!)

1 1. The Israelis launch in the evening of 29 October 1956 a large scale attack on the Egyptian forces with the aim of reaching the Canal zone the following day.

   2. On being apprised of these events, the British and French
5 Governments during the day of 30 October 1956 respectively and simultaneously make two appeals to the Egyptian Government and the Israeli Government on the following lines:

   A To the Egyptian Government
   a) halt all acts of war.
10 b) withdraw all its troops ten miles from the Canal.
   c) accept temporary occupation of key positions on the Canal by the Anglo-French forces to guarantee freedom of passage though the Canal by vessels of all nations until a final settlement.
15 B To the Israeli Government
   a) halt all acts of war.

b) withdraw all its troops ten miles to the east of the Canal ...
3. In the event that the Egyptian Government should fail to agree
within the stipulated time the conditions of the appeal addressed to
20 it, the Anglo-French forces will launch military operations against
the Egyptian forces in the early hours of the morning of 31
October.

The plan, while providing Britain with an excuse for intervention, did
have a number of major snags which should have been apparent, with
any degree of foresight, in October 1956. To imagine that the collusion
between Britain, France and Israel could be kept secret was clearly naive
in the extreme. Moreover, Britain's Arab allies were hardly likely to look
kindly upon a British attack arranged in advance with Israel. There was
also the uncomfortable fact that the USA was still opposed to military
intervention and had not been informed of the Sèvres Protocol. This was
serious because Eden had had warnings from the Treasury that the
strength of the pound sterling was too fragile for Britain to go it alone
without US backing. The knowledge that the main operations would
take place in the immediate run-up to the American Presidential
elections may have influenced Eden's thinking. Perhaps he thought the
USA would be too preoccupied to react effectively or that Eisenhower's
administration would not wish to act in a manner hostile to Israel lest it
should alienate the large Jewish vote in America. Eden and most British
policy-makers seemed to have assumed that in the last analysis
Eisenhower would not let Britain down. The Chancellor of the
Exchequer Harold Macmillan, who had recently met Eisenhower in
America, seems to have encouraged this view.

8 Suez: October-November 1956

On 29 October the Sèvres plan was put into operation with Israeli forces
overrunning Egyptian forces in the Sinai desert. The next day Britain
and France issued ultimata requiring Israel and Egypt to cease warlike
action and withdraw to positions ten miles clear of the Suez Canal.
Egypt was further required to allow Anglo-French forces to occupy
positions at Suez, Port Said and Ismailia. Both countries were given
twelve hours to comply, otherwise Britain and France would forcefully
intervene. Israel (naturally) agreed. Egypt (as anticipated) refused. On
31 October British and French bombers struck Egyptian airfields,
virtually destroying the Egyptian airforce but not bombing on anything
like the scale necessary to break Egypt's will to resist. Then came delay
as the Anglo-French invasion force, which had been assembled at Malta,
made its way slowly across the Mediterranean ready for sea borne
landings on 6 November. In retaliation the Egyptians blocked the Suez
Canal and ensured that oil pipe-lines through Syria were cut.
    In Britain and around the world, the Anglo-French attack caused an

enormous furore. In the House of Commons, the debate over Suez was violent. Many Labour MPs suspected that there had been collusion between Britain, France and Israel. The government denied this. On 31 October, Selwyn Lloyd, said in the Commons:

1 It is quite wrong to state that Israel was incited to this action by her Majesty's government. There was no prior agreement between us about it. It is of course true that the Israeli mobilisation gave some advance warning, and we urged restraint upon the Israeli
5 Government and in particular drew attention to the serious consequences of any attack on Jordan.

The vast majority of Conservative MPs supported Eden's action and the government won a large majority on an Opposition censure motion. However, there were a few Conservative abstentions and two junior ministers resigned. The country was clearly divided over the Suez operation. The lack of firm domestic support may have undermined Eden's will to fight. But on the other hand opinion polls seemed to indicate that most British people supported military action and Eden derived comfort from a letter of approval from Churchill.

Most foreign governments condemned the Anglo-French action. Russian criticism came as no surprise. Russia's main concern, however, was the crisis in Hungary, which developed independently but at almost exactly the same time as Suez. At the end of October the Hungarian people rose in revolt against their Russian-backed communist government. The Russians sent in tanks to crush the insurgents and a new hard-line communist government was imposed on Hungary. There was great sympathy in the West for Hungary but a general realisation that little could be done to help the Hungarians without the risk of an all out war with Russia. Events in Hungary and Suez increased world tension but had relatively little - direct - effect on each other.

More important than Russian opposition was the fact that President Eisenhower condemned the Suez invasion out of hand. Eisenhower's anger was understandable. He had made clear his opposition to the use of force from the start and the crisis occurred at an inconvenient moment in the Presidential election campaign, possibly damaging Eisenhower's chances. Eisenhower also resented the fact that he had been deceived by his closest ally. The extent of Eisenhower's opposition took Eden by surprise.

In the United Nations most countries, including several members of the Commonwealth (especially India), were critical of British action. An American resolution calling for an immediate ceasefire passed by 64 votes to 5 (Britain, France, Israel, New Zealand and Australia). This verdict did not easily match Britain's contention that her forces were acting as policeman on behalf of the world body. Only by using her veto power on the Security Council, was Britain able to block United Nations calls for an immediate ceasefire. On 3 November Britain abstained in the vote on a Canadian resolution for a United Nations Emergency Force to garrison the Canal.

On 5 November Anglo-French paratroopers landed near Port Said in Egypt. On the same day the USSR issued threats hinting that it might send Soviet 'volunteers' to help Egypt and might even launch a missile attack on London and Paris if the invasion was not called off. These threats probably had little effect. (The British government guessed the Russians were bluffing and knew that in the event of a Russian attack Britain could count on US support.) Far more important was American action. In early November US financial pressure led to a run on the pound and a 15 per cent loss of Britain's gold and dollar reserves. The Chancellor Harold Macmillan, previously a 'hawk', lost his nerve and decided that Britain could not afford to go on with the Suez adventure.

On 6 November the Anglo-French sea borne forces finally landed in Egypt. From a military point of view the operation, involving 45,000 British troops, was a great success. Twenty miles of the Canal was quickly occupied and casualties were light. The whole of the Canal could probably have been occupied within a week. However, Egypt and Israel now accepted a ceasefire. Israel had achieved all her military objectives and the Egyptians thought they might have better luck with an international tribunal than by continuing to fight. This ceasefire removed all pretext for the Anglo-French invasion. Convinced by Macmillan that Britain faced financial ruin, Eden determined to abort the Suez operation. In an effort to save some face, he announced he was now ready to support the Canadian idea for a United Nations Emergency Force to garrison the Canal, and ordered a ceasefire to commence at midnight on 6 November. The French had little alternative but to follow suit.

Eden remained reasonably optimistic arguing that Britain still held a strong bargaining position that could be exploited in negotiation. However, these hopes soon died. Eisenhower insisted on a complete Anglo-French withdrawal before the US would offer any financial support. American pressure only had such a dramatic effect because of the determination on Britain's part not to devalue the pound. The fear was that this would lead to the destruction of sterling's international position. The government decided, in effect, to sacrifice its Middle Eastern policy to its sterling policy. On 28-29 November Macmillan persuaded a demoralised Cabinet (with Eden now absent ill) that Britain must withdraw - unconditionally. Eisenhower refused to allow Britain and France to unblock the Canal and forbad them to take any part in the United Nations peace-keeping force which was set up to police the Egyptian-Israeli frontier. Only after all Anglo-French troops had withdrawn was he prepared to give US support for sterling. By the end of 1956 all British and French troops had left Egypt. Not until April 1957 was the Canal finally unblocked and arrangements agreed for its future management.

9 The Results of Suez

On 19 November 1956 Eden, suffering from severe overstrain, departed for Jamaica to recuperate. His health deteriorated further and on 9 January 1957 he resigned. Given the Suez debacle, his resignation was possibly inevitable. Given the fact that he told a deliberate lie in the House of Commons about the extent of Britain's collusion with Israel, it was also probably just. Most historians view Suez as an unqualified disaster. Michael Foot, a Labour MP at the time of Suez, wrote in 1975:

1 Instead of opening the Canal, it was blocked; instead of saving British lives and property, they had been put at Nasser's mercy; instead of toppling Nasser, he was enthroned; instead of keeping the oil flowing, it was soon to be rationed; instead of winning
5 friends, we had lost them ... the expedition had achieved the exact opposite of the Government's declared intention.

These charges are difficult to answer. Eden, warned by the Treasury that a costly military operation was likely to give sterling holders the jitters, had over-estimated Britain's power. Moreover he had fatally misjudged America's reaction to his military operation. As a result, he achieved none of his objectives. Nasser emerged from the crisis as the pre-eminent leader of Arab nationalism and Britain's prestige had been seriously damaged both in the Middle East and throughout the world.

However, Eden has some sympathisers who think the Suez crisis was understandable, given the prevailing belief that Britain was still a great power. It can also be said, in Eden's defence, that ill-health throughout the crisis might have impaired his judgement. Resting in Jamaica, he was virtually cut off from the decisions of late November. Some historians have tried to shift the blame by spreading more widely the responsibility for the decisions to go ahead and then to stop. Macmillan, who strongly supported the operation at first but who then lost heart when the going got tough, would certainly seem to deserve some blame. Most Cabinet members fully supported Eden's policies. Few British policymakers expected the intensity of the American reaction, both in leading opposition in the United Nations and in failing to support the pound.

The US government was blamed by many Conservatives at the time for letting down its closest ally. Dulles has also been attacked for hinting - in private - that he might support force, thus encouraging British action. But the notion of 'American perfidy' should not be taken too far. Eisenhower had said all along that he opposed the use of force. In the end the fatal errors were British, and most of them were Eden's. Churchill commented later that had he still been in office he was certain that, 'I wouldn't have done anything without consulting the Americans'. There is still some support for the view that if Eden had used force immediately he might have presented the world with a fait accompli. However, British forces were in no position to act speedily at the time. There was a shortage of battle-ready troops and adequate air and sea transport. Others claim that if Eden had ignored American and United Nations pressure, success might well have been attainable. Churchill is reported to have said, 'I am not sure I should have dared to start, but I am sure I should not have dared to stop'. Certainly from a military point of view the events from 31 October to 6 November went well.

However, exactly what Eden expected to do with the Canal, if it had been secured, seems not to have been sufficiently thought through. Although secret discussions had gone on between Britain and some Egyptian politicians, Eden's hope that Nasser might be overthrown and replaced by a new pro-British Egyptian government seems incredible. Nor does it seem likely that Britain or France could have held Egypt down by force.

The Suez operation was an aberration from key post-war British policies. Collusion with Israel conflicted spectacularly with the search for new partnerships with the Arabs. Allying with France and ignoring America went against all British policy since 1945 and cast doubt over the future of the 'special relationship'. British collusion with France and Israel was Eden's brainchild and it is hard to understand how the Prime Minister could have convinced himself that world opinion could ever be deceived. Suez was a sad end to Eden's long and generally honourable career. It is somewhat ironic that the cause of his failure lay not in domestic politics (in which he lacked experience and finesse) but in his handling of foreign affairs - supposedly his metier.

Much has been written about the results of the Suez crisis. Some historians have seen it a major event in modern British history - a watershed, separating the years in which Britain's survival as an independent world power seemed possible (and desirable), from the years after - which saw the rapid end of Empire and the scaling down of Britain's global commitments. However, other historians have viewed Suez as little more than a melodramatic episode, which merely exposed underlying and obvious trends in the decline of British power.

Certainly Suez had some important results. It helped bring about a change of Prime Minister. It diverted world attention from Hungary and robbed the West of exploiting a useful moral advantage over communism. The cost of Suez to British standing throughout the Middle East was high. Pro-British regimes in the region were seriously embarrassed and weakened. Jordan felt bound to denounce her treaty with Britain. British influence in Iraq faded and in 1958 a government similar in background to that in Egypt came to power. Nasser became an Arab - and indeed Third World - hero and encouraged Arab nationalists and anti-colonial nationalists elsewhere. Britain's international prestige suffered. The Commonwealth had shown itself to be less solid, and less susceptible to British guidance, than many had imagined. For an

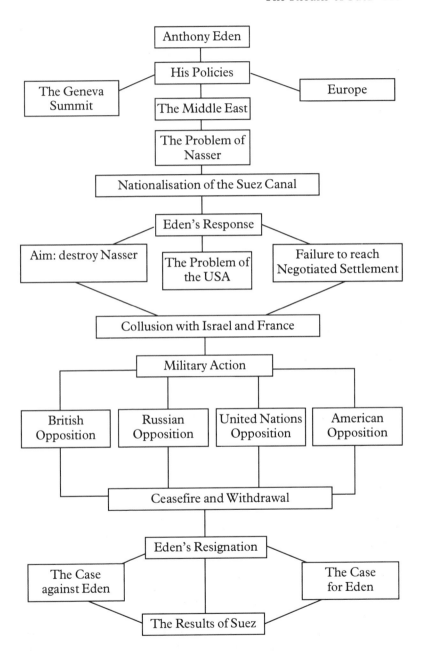

Summary - Anthony Eden and Suez, 1955-6

Egyptian ex-colonel to twist the lion's tail and get away with it, was also a hard blow to Britain's self-esteem.

Nevertheless perhaps the results of Suez should not be exaggerated. Eden's departure apart, Suez had relatively little impact on politics in Britain. If anything the crisis reunited the Conservative Party which went on to win the 1959 election. Relations with America were quickly restored. Many people in Britain had begun to question the nature of Britain's world role long before Suez. It is too easy and too simple to see the accelerated colonial withdrawal after 1960 as the direct consequence of the humiliation of 1956. Arguably Suez did not trigger off an imperial explosion but at most simply gave a push to causes which were already in motion.

Making notes on 'Anthony Eden and Suez, 1955-6'

Your notes on this chapter should give you an understanding of the causes, events and consequences of the Suez crisis. Anthony Eden is invariably blamed for his mishandling of the crisis. (He is somewhat unfortunate in that he tends to be remembered for this one failure and not for his numerous achievements!) You need to have an understanding of why Eden, a man with great diplomatic experience, acted as he did. You should also have opinions, supported by evidence, about whether he was wise or foolish to act as he did. As you read the chapter try to identify what Eden and Britain could have done that was different. Should Eden have allowed Nasser to get away with nationalising the Suez Canal? Should he have tried to work more closely with the USA? Should he have attacked Egypt sooner? Should he have ignored financial pressure and remained in Egypt?

Answering essay questions on 'Anthony Eden and Suez, 1955-6'

It is highly unlikely that you will be asked for either a narrative of the events of Eden's premiership or a description of the Suez crisis. More likely you will need to use evidence from this chapter to answer specific questions about Eden's role in the Suez crisis. Two typical examples of such questions are:

1 Account for Britain's involvement - and failure - in the Suez crisis.
2 'I am not sure I should have dared to start, but I am sure I should not have dared to stop.' Comment on Churchill's view of the Suez crisis.

Question 2 looks - and probably is - the most difficult. However, the two questions are not dissimilar. In both cases you will need to comment on the reasons why Britain got involved at Suez and why she ultimately backed down. Put the main causes for British involvement into some sort of 'rank order'. Then place the main reasons for Britain's defeat in a similar 'rank order'. You now have got the 'meat' of both essays. However, the introductions and conclusions of these two questions are likely to be very different. Write down a possible introductory paragraph for both questions. In what ways are they different? In what ways are they the same? Now do exactly the same with the concluding paragraphs. Remember that while at the start of an essay you may outline an argument, in the conclusion you must be much more precise - and must answer the set question.

Source-based questions on 'Anthony Eden and Suez', 1955-6

1 Eden and America
Read Eden's comment on America in October 1955 on page 103. Answer the following questions:
a) What interests, apart from oil, did Britain have in the Middle East? (3 marks)
b) What might be said, with hindsight, in support of Eden's statement? (3 marks)
c) With hindsight, what might be said against Eden's views? (4 marks)

2 Responses to Suez Nationalisation
Read Eden's, Kirkpatrick's and Lennox-Boyd's views of the Suez situation in July-August 1956 on page 106. Answer the following questions:
a) Why did Eden regard the Suez Canal as a matter of 'the widest international importance'? (3 marks)
b) In what way might Eden have envisaged Britain being able to 'take advantage' of the situation? (3 marks)
c) What was Kirkpatrick's main argument and to what extent was it consistent with Eden's views? (3 marks)
d) What arguments, with the benefit of hindsight, might be made against the views expressed in the three extracts? (6 marks)

3 British Collusion
Read the extract from the Protocol of Sèvres and Selwyn Lloyd's speech to the House of Commons (pages 109-10 & 111). Answer the following questions:
a) Why do you think the official copies of the Protocol have never come to light? (3 marks)
b) Did Britain, France and Israel expect Egypt to accept the Anglo-French demands? Explain your answer. (3 marks)
c) To what extent were the agreements reached at Sèvres actually carried out? (5 marks)
d) Comment on Selwyn Lloyd's statement that, 'There was no prior agreement between us'. (5 marks)
e) Why might Lloyd have expressed concern about an Israeli attack on Jordan? (4 marks)

CHAPTER 7

The Wind of Change, 1957-64

1 Harold Macmillan

In January 1957 most people expected that R.A. Butler, effectively leader since Eden's health had collapsed in November 1956, would become Prime Minister. However, many right-wing Conservatives considered Butler too moderate and Lord Salisbury and Churchill advised the Queen that Harold Macmillan should become Prime Minister.

Although Macmillan lacked Butler's experience, he seemed a 'safe' candidate who might unite the right and left wings of the Conservative Party. Born in 1894, educated at Eton and Oxford, he had gone into his father's publishing business before serving (bravely) in the Grenadier Guards during the First World War. In the 1930s, he had criticised his own party for appeasement and for its failure to do more for the unemployed. He had served Churchill in the 1950s, first as Minister of Housing and then as Minister of Defence. After a few months at the Foreign Office, he became Chancellor of the Exchequer under Eden. Remarkably Macmillan escaped blame for Suez, despite the fact that he had, in Harold Wilson's words, been 'first in, first out'.

Macmillan was a complex personality: sensitive and cynical; compassionate and ruthless; privately shy but publicly self-confident: a fascinating mix of professional politician, amateur country gentleman, and great performer - particularly on television, fast developing as an essential means of political communication. Though often nervous and highly strung, he had the gift of appearing cool and unflappable and unlike Eden was never overwhelmed by work, for which he had a great appetite. He quickly established his authority over his Cabinet colleagues, soon won a great political ascendancy in the Commons and thoroughly enjoyed the exercise of power.

His main concern in 1957 was to revive the flagging fortunes of both his country and his party after the humiliation of Suez. He succeeded in doing both. In the October 1959 General Election the Conservatives won their third victory in a row and actually increased their majority. This victory was essentially a testament to 'Super Mac's' perceived success on the home front. Many believed, as Macmillan boasted, that they had 'never had it so good'. However, Macmillan's skilful handling of diplomatic affairs and a feeling that he had restored Britain's shattered prestige contributed to his electoral triumph.

Like Churchill and Eden, Macmillan saw foreign affairs as of vital importance and was determined to play an important role on the world stage. His own Foreign Secretary (on the major issues), he was to become one of the most travelled British Prime Ministers. He appeared to have similar aims to his two Conservative predecessors. 'We are a great world power', he told the Commons in May 1957, 'and we intend to remain so'. He had no intention of apologising for Suez (and never did!). Almost as an act of defiance to the world, he kept Selwyn Lloyd as Foreign Secretary. In 1957 he seemed opposed to any idea of Britain joining a federated Europe and seemed keen to maintain the Empire/Commonwealth connection. Above all, Macmillan was determined to rebuild the 'special relationship' with the USA which had been seriously damaged by the Suez fiasco. Half-American himself, Macmillan believed that the common interests of both Britain and the USA would be better served by collaboration than by mutual recrimination. The Soviet threat, underlined by events in Hungary in 1956, remained serious enough to merit a rapid restoration of good Anglo-American relations. Although determined to stand firm against the communist threat, Macmillan hoped that there might be an opportunity to improve relations with the USSR and was particularly keen to reach some agreement on nuclear disarmament. He realised this was unlikely to be easy. Khrushchev, now unchallenged ruler in Russia, was brash and unpredictable and seemed determined to bully, possibly with the intention of testing the resolve of the Western alliance.

2 Relations with the USA and USSR, 1957-60

Macmillan immediately set about trying to patch up relations with America. In March 1957 he met President Eisenhower in Bermuda. The two men had been wartime colleagues in North Africa and their conversations were conducted in a relaxed and friendly manner. The special relationship, to Macmillan's delight, was quickly re-established. Eisenhower agreed to the stationing of 60 American Thor missiles on British soil under a joint (or 'dual-key') firing arrangement. At a further meeting with Macmillan in Washington in October 1957, Eisenhower promised that he would press Congress to repeal the 1946 Macmahon Act which forbad the exchange of atomic information with any other country including Britain. This was done in 1958 and led to a complete restoration of nuclear information exchanges between Britain and America. The US decision to share her nuclear technology with Britain (no other country was given such treatment) indicated America's intention to heal the rift over Suez and reaffirmed the fact that the Anglo-American partnership remained at the heart of Europe's defence. Nuclear sharing would have been inconceivable without the highest levels of mutual trust enjoyed by the political and military establishments of both countries.

Macmillan's skill in rebuilding the Anglo-American alliance could not conceal a decisive shift in the relative positions of Britain and the USA. Before Suez, independent British action without US approval still seemed possible. Large parts of the non-communist world, and particularly the Middle East, still lay under British rather than American influence. But the years after 1957 saw the steady expansion of US power and her entry into regions previously reserved to British (or French) influence.

This was true in Africa where there was a steady growth of American diplomatic activity and a five-fold increase of American economic aid between 1958 and 1963. It was true in South-Eastern Asia where the USA was drawn more directly into the politics of Laos and Vietnam. It was also true in the Middle East where the US was now prepared to play a much greater role. Failure at Suez and the fact that she had co-operated with Israel combined to undermine Britain's position in the Arab world. Nasser's example provided inspiration for a number of attempts to subvert the Western-dominated status quo.

The so-called Eisenhower Doctrine of 1957 asserted American concern for the security of the Middle East. Henceforward if nations of the Middle East were threatened 'by alien forces hostile to freedom', they could request American aid. In May 1958 US marines landed in Beirut to protect the Lebanese government. In July 1958 British paratroopers, with US approval, were dropped into Jordan to help King Hussain maintain his position following the overthrow of the pro-British regime in Iraq. British and American actions had some success in ensuring that Western influence in the Middle East was not destroyed.

Russia seemed an increasing threat. Khrushchev was keen to exert Russian influence in the so-called 'Third World' and actively supported national liberation movements. The USSR, which appeared to be growing in strength, seemed a good model for ex-colonial countries to follow. In October 1957 Russia launched Sputnik, the first artificial earth satellite. The following month Sputnik 2, which contained a dog called Laika, was sent into orbit. Americans, were alarmed by this striking proof of Russia's scientific and technological progress and its obvious potential to develop missiles of intercontinental range. (Macmillan noted in his diary that most people in Britain were probably more concerned with the plight of the dog!)

Khrushchev adopted an aggressive posture to the West. In November 1958 he issued an ultimatum demanding the withdrawal of Allied forces within six months from West Berlin which would become a demilitarised free city. This threat prompted Macmillan to visit Moscow in February 1959 to see what Khrushchev was up to. The visit - the first by a major western leader since 1945 - resulted in a great deal of plain-speaking which perhaps helped reduce east-west tension. Although a Foreign Ministers Conference at Geneva in May 1959 failed to reach any solutions to the Berlin problem, Khrushchev's six months ultimatum passed with no dire consequences, and in September 1959 Khrushchev, on a visit to the USA, withdrew the ultimatum.

However, a Summit meeting in Paris in May 1960 broke up almost before it had begun after the shooting down of an American U-2 spy plane over Russian territory. Khrushchev denounced US policy and demanded an apology, which Eisenhower refused to give. Thereupon the Soviet delegation walked out of the Conference - to Macmillan's bitter disappointment. The war of words over Berlin continued and there was a new 'ice age' in East-West relations. Macmillan strongly supported most aspects of American policy. In September 1960 he confronted Khrushchev in the United Nations Assembly. During Macmillan's speech, Khrushchev, after a series of oafish interruptions, began banging one of his shoes on a desk. Macmillan stopped and asked quietly, 'Mr President, perhaps we can have a translation, I can not quite follow'. The remark discomforted Khrushchev and gave Macmillan a reputation for style in the USA.

3 British Defence Policy

By 1957 most experts were aware that Britain was spending more than it could really afford on defence - particularly at a time when British industry was facing tough competition from Germany and Japan. The shortages of equipment of every kind which the Suez preparations had revealed led the government to question whether the large expenditure of the previous few years on conventional warfare capabilities had been money well spent. In 1957 Macmillan appointed Duncan Sandys, (Churchill's son-in-law) as Minister of Defence with the job of cutting defence spending. Macmillan, aware of the likely resistance within the armed services, assured Sandys that he could rely on his full support.

The April 1957 White Paper on Defence, which laid down the basis for future defence policy, drew together various threads in British thinking which had emerged in the 1950s. The following extract indicates some of the thinking behind the main proposals:

1 Britain's defence policy is determined by her obligation to make her contribution to NATO and her other alliances for collective defence, as well as to discharge her own special responsibilities in many parts of the world ...
5   3. However, the time has now come to revise not merely the size, but the whole character of the defence plan. The Communist threat remains, but its nature has changed; and it is now evident that, on both military and economic grounds, it is necessary to make a fresh appreciation of the problem and to adopt a new
10 approach towards it.
        4. In recent years military technology has been making dramatic strides ... In less than a decade, the atom bomb dropped at Hiroshima has been overtaken by the far more powerful hydrogen or megaton bomb. Parallel with this, the evolution of rocket
15 weapons of all kinds, both offensive and defensive, has been proceeding apace.

5. It has been clear for some time that these scientific advances must fundamentally alter the whole basis of military planning ...

7. Over the last five years, defence has on average absorbed 10%
20 of Britain's gross national product. Some 7% of the working population are either in the Services or supporting them. One-eighth of the output of the metal-using industries, upon which the export trade so largely depends, is devoted to defence.
25 An undue proportion of qualified scientists and engineers are engaged on military work. In addition, the retention of such large forces abroad gives rise to heavy charges which place a severe strain upon the balance of payments ...

15. The free world is to-day mainly dependent for its protection
30 upon the nuclear capacity of the United States. While Britain cannot by comparison make more than a modest contribution, there is a wide measure of agreement that she must possess an appreciable element of nuclear deterrent power of her own.

The White Paper argued that the main focus of Britain's defence should be the nuclear bomb. The forthcoming testing of a British H-bomb (it was successfully tested in May 1957) and the coming into service of a fleet of Vulcan bombers capable of reaching Moscow, enabled Sandys to emphasise the nuclear deterrent with greater confidence than his predecessors. Conventional forces were to be cut from 690,000 (in 1957) to 375,000 (in 1962). Conscription was to be abandoned by 1960. Overall Britain's defence spending was to be cut from 10 per cent to 7 per cent of gross national product by 1962.

The government's new defence policy met with little opposition at first. Most Conservatives were totally committed to the nuclear deterrent believing that it would enable Britain to remain a world power on the cheap. The Labour leader Hugh Gaitskell supported nuclear weapons. So did Aneurin Bevan, darling of the Labour left. He told the 1957 Labour Party Conference that without the nuclear deterrent British influence in the world would disappear and claimed that if Britain did not possess a nuclear bomb, British Foreign Secretary's henceforward would be sent 'naked into the Conference chamber'. However, many Labour Party activists wanted Britain to renounce the H-bomb. Some joined the Campaign for Nuclear Disarmament (CND), set up in February 1958 and soon organising protest marches from London to the Atomic Weapon's research establishment at Aldermaston.

However, Macmillan's government was not particularly troubled by CND. The main defence problem continued to be that of cost. The government, with much the same obligations after 1957 as before, found it hard to cut back spending on conventional forces. The costs of nuclear defence also began to escalate in a way not envisaged in 1957. No sooner was the V-bomber force developed than it became obsolete because of improved missile technology. Attempts to develop a ground-to-ground missile - Blue Streak - proved too costly and the project was abandoned in February 1960.

In June 1960, after three months of intense negotiation, Macmillan secured agreement that Britain could purchase the American Skybolt air-to-ground missile which was being developed for the United States air force. This could be fired by V-bombers at a longer distance from the target and was therefore less vulnerable to Russian anti-aircraft defences. Skybolt was to be solely at Britain's disposal. The fact that the USA would bear all the development costs involved in the project meant that there were substantial financial savings for Britain. In return, Britain agreed to make a base available in Scotland for 'Polaris', the new submarine-launched missile which the USA was also developing. Informally Eisenhower agreed that if anything went wrong with Skybolt, Britain could have Polaris.

4 Macmillan and Kennedy

After his close association with Eisenhower, Macmillan feared for relations with John F. Kennedy who became the new American President in 1961. Despite differences of age and style, the two leaders soon built up a friendly relationship. Macmillan said, 'I was sort of son to Ike, and it was the other way round with Kennedy'. Kennedy put it differently: 'I feel at home with Macmillan because I can share my loneliness with him. The others are all foreigners to me'. Kennedy often welcomed Macmillan's advice and was happy to use him as a sounding board for his ideas. The appointment of David Ormsby Gore, an old Kennedy friend, as British ambassador to Washington, helped maintain British influence in America. The fact that Cold War tensions showed no sign of lessening further strengthened Anglo-American relations.

Kennedy, very much a Cold War warrior, was determined to revitalise America and to counter communism. His Presidency, however, got off to a bad start. In April 1960 an American-backed attempt to overthrow Fidel Castro, the pro-Russian leader of Cuba, failed miserably at the Bay of Pigs. This debacle probably convinced Khrushchev that the 43-year-old President was a bungling amateur who could be pushed about. In June 1961 Kennedy met Khrushchev in Vienna. The talks ended acrimoniously. Problems in Berlin were not resolved and East-West tensions remained acute. In August 1961, Khrushchev, aiming to stop the flood of refugees from East Germany, ordered the building of the Berlin Wall, sealing off all access from the east to the western sectors of the city. This draconian solution proved effective and the crisis passed. Macmillan won Kennedy's respect for strongly supporting the USA throughout the Berlin crisis.

By the early 1960s Russia, which put the first man in space in April 1961, seemed to be gaining the technological edge. However Kennedy's talk (in the 1960 election) of a 'missile gap' between the USA and the USSR was a myth. The USA, in fact, had a great superiority and that superiority increased after 1961. This knowledge gave Kennedy increased confidence in his dealings with Khrushchev.

In October 1962 US aerial reconnaissance revealed evidence of the installation of medium range ground-to-ground missiles in Cuba, supervised by Russian technicians. Soviet missiles on Cuba would help redress the nuclear balance and Kennedy immediately demanded that the missiles be removed. Rather than invade Cuba, he imposed a naval blockade around the island and made it clear that vessels carrying missiles would be turned back. As Russian ships neared the blockade zone, the world stood on the brink of nuclear war. In the end, however, the Russian ships turned away and Khrushchev agreed to remove Soviet missiles from Cuba in return for Kennedy promising not to invade the island.

The Cuban crisis dramatised the international dominance of the superpowers and the fact that Britain was not in the same league. According to some left-wing critics, America's disregard of Britain's views demonstrated the irrelevance of Macmillan's world role posturings and the weakness of the special relationship. Throughout the crisis, however, Kennedy did seek advice from Macmillan and the two leaders had a series of long telephone calls. At the end of October Kennedy thanked Macmillan for his 'heartening support', adding that 'our daily conversations have been of inestimable value in these past days'. Macmillan later wrote, 'We were 'in on' and took full part in (and almost responsibility for) every American move. Our complete calm helped keep the Europeans calm'. On the other hand, Ormsby Gore, who on his own initiative had persuaded Kennedy to take certain significant decisions, commented, 'I can't honestly think of anything said from London that changed the US action'. Kennedy had taken the crucial decisions before consulting Macmillan. The crisis showed that in the last analysis, an American President, not the British government, could decide the fate of Britain.

Both sides had been shaken by the nearness of nuclear war. This led to an improvement in Soviet-American relations and helped pave the way for a Nuclear Test Ban Treaty in August 1963, banning all atmospheric nuclear tests. This was the most significant measure of disarmament achieved since 1945. Macmillan could be proud of the measure for he had sought it longer and with greater zeal than any other statesman.

In the autumn of 1962 it seemed that Britain's status as a nuclear power was in jeopardy. In November 1962 the USA announced that it intended to scrap Skybolt, the missile Britain intended to buy. Senior American officials, fearing that British nuclear possession could only encourage nuclear proliferation, wanted to use the opportunity to eliminate Britain as a nuclear power. At a meeting with Kennedy at

Nassau in the Bahamas in December 1962, Macmillan demanded that America provide a substitute for Skybolt. Kennedy, impressed with the fervour with which Macmillan put his case, overrode his advisers and agreed to supply Britain with the USA's latest Polaris submarine-launched missile system.

The Polaris deal was represented by Macmillan, with some justification, as a major diplomatic victory. Britain, alone among America's allies, was allowed to buy the latest US nuclear technology at a remarkably generous price. Polaris, which would have British warheads and be fired from British submarines, confirmed Britain's status as a nuclear power for the foreseeable future. However Harold Wilson, the new Labour leader, maintained that the so-called independent British nuclear deterrent was neither independent, nor British, nor even a deterrent and pledged that a Labour government would renegotiate the Nassau Agreement. In many ways, however, the most important critic of the Polaris deal was the French President Charles de Gaulle. The purchase of Polaris occurred at the same time that the French were embarking on production of their own - genuine - independent nuclear deterrent. Rather than becoming increasingly dependent on America, Britain might have been better trying to work in co-operation with France on nuclear technology, thus demonstrating her European credentials.

5 Decolonisation

a) Macmillan and Empire

In 1957 Britain still controlled important areas in Africa, Asia and the West Indies. Between 1948 and 1957 only three British colonies had become independent - Sudan (1956), the Gold Coast (1957) and Malaya (1957). Between 1957 and 1964, however, (and especially between 1960 and 1963), the British overseas Empire effectively came to an end. By 1964 Britain was left with a handful of territories which, for the most part, were considered too small to be viable as independent nations. Few Empires have disappeared so swiftly, so completely and with so little armed conflict. Historians continue to debate why this process occurred.

In 1957 Macmillan appears to have had no plans for an abrupt and complete withdrawal from Empire - although he did wonder whether he was 'destined to be the remodeller or the liquidator of Empire'. Like many British politicians, he wanted to hand over power only when colonies were ready and able to administer themselves. To hand over power prematurely would be to betray Britain's responsibility to the native populations.

In 1957 a Cabinet Colonial Policy Committee was set up to review the costs of Empire. It came up with mixed findings, judging that overall economic considerations were fairly evenly balanced with expenditure savings here being offset by reduced commercial or strategic advantage there. It concluded that:

> 1 Any premature withdrawal of authority by the United Kingdom would seem bound to add to the areas of stress and discontent in the world . . . The United Kingdom has been too long connected with its Colonial possessions to sever ties abruptly without creating
> 5 a bewilderment which would be discreditable and dangerous.

By the end of 1959, however, Macmillan seems to have become convinced that the leisurely programme for the transferring of power envisaged by the Colonial Office, particularly in Africa, would no longer do. Many commentators have seen the appointment of Iain Macleod as Colonial Secretary in October 1959 as an indication of a change of policy on Macmillan's part. Macleod, unlike previous Colonial Secretaries, sympathised with African aspirations and favoured rapid decolonisation. However, it is still not clear whether Macleod acted largely on his own initiative or applied principles which had been laid down for him by Macmillan. Those historians who see Macmillan as the puppeteer, planning and directing the change of colonial policy, usually regard the 1959 general election as a crucial factor. They claim that a host of younger, more liberal Conservative MPs entered the House of Commons, submerging older reactionary elements who had sentimental attachments to Empire and to white settlers. This is seen as giving Macmillan his opportunity.

Certainly Macmillan had tremendous authority over all aspects of British external policy by the autumn of 1959 - and his sympathies were increasingly on the side of the black Africans. However, his impact on colonial policy should not be exaggerated. Many British policy-makers in both the Cabinet, Foreign Office and Colonial Office held similar views to Macmillan and it is not clear who convinced who. Nor is it certain that Macmillan (or Macleod) had any real idea of where they were going in Africa or in any other colonial territory. Nor does it seem that there was ever a general Cabinet decision to withdraw quickly from Empire. Rather than adopting a common policy indiscriminately, Macmillan's government seems to have taken account of political conditions that varied greatly from colony to colony.

However, the speed of change after 1959 (especially in Africa) and the consistency of its direction, indicates that something more than just a haphazard series of pragmatic responses to local conditions was at work. What caused Macmillan's government to change policy?

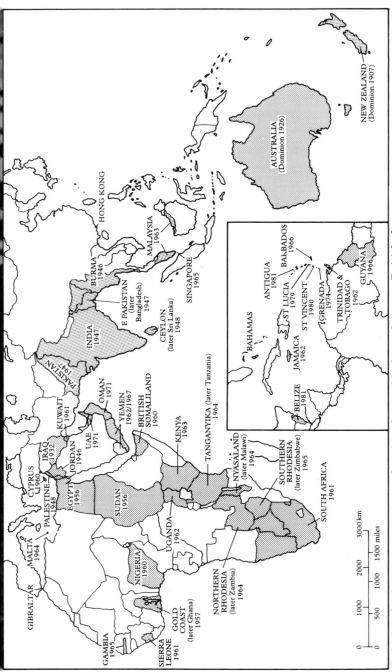

British colonies or protectorates, showing dates of independence or British departure (inset showing the central part of America)

b) The Situation in Africa, 1959-60

The upsurge of more determined nationalist sentiment within Britain's colonies was certainly an important factor. Throughout Africa nationalist organisations won increasing support and seemed ready to use active and possibly violent resistance to imperial rule. Macmillan's conviction of the strength of African nationalism deepened as a result of a six week tour to Africa in 1960. Speaking to the South African Parliament in Cape Town in 1960, Macmillan said:

1 Fifteen years ago this movement [nationalism] spread through Asia. Many countries there of different races and civilisations pressed their claims to an independent national life. Today the same thing is happening in Africa. The most striking of all
5 impressions I have formed since I left London a month ago is of the strength of this African national consciousness. In different places it may take different forms, but it is happening everywhere. The wind of change is blowing through this continent. Whether we like it or not this growth of national consciousness is a political fact . . .
10 our national policies must take account of it.

It was not just British colonial rule which was threatened by the upsurge in nationalist activity in Africa. France and Belgium also faced challenges. The prolonged French struggle to keep Algeria had finally resulted in the fall of the Fourth French Republic. The new French President, Charles de Gaulle, finally offered Algeria full independence. He then made similar offers to most of France's African colonies. In 1960 Belgium followed France's example and decided to pull out of the Congo.

Britain could not ignore France and Belgium's African policies. As one country was granted independence, others increased their demands and it became more difficult to sustain a case for delay elsewhere. In 1960 no less than 16 new African states entered the United Nations, changing the balance of its membership. These newly independent states pressed for independence for other colonial territories. Britain, previously the pioneer of devolution, was left in the embarrassing position of seeming more illiberal than the rest of Europe. Moreover it was hard to justify denial of independence to British colonies whose size, economic and political development far outstripped that of France's former colonies. Pressure on Britain became more urgent as the Congo exploded into anarchy and civil war after June 1960. There seemed a real possibility that trouble might spread into one or more of the British colonies bordering the Congo.

However, the view that nationalism swept the board and made the collapse of colonial rule inevitable is too simplistic. The strength of the nationalist movements has sometimes been exaggerated. Not all nationalist leaders won the hearts and minds of their people, although afterwards they often claimed they had! Within virtually all of Britain's African colonies there were great differences of interest and identity. In most colonies there was the fear that if independence came, power would be seized by one tribe, region or religious group. Britain, therefore, was in a position to play off one group against another as she had done effectively in the past. She could also hope for support from conservative vested interest groups within the colonies if there was a real threat of social upheaval. Moreover, in the last resort Britain almost certainly had the military power to at least hold the nationalist movements in check. Portugal, a far weaker power, was able to hold on to her colonies for much longer than Britain and white minority regimes in Southern Rhodesia and South Africa had some success in maintaining power after 1964. What was lacking in Britain was not so much the strength to crush the nationalist movements as the will to maintain colonial rule. There were several reasons for this.

Macmillan appreciated by 1960 that any action, other than a rapid devolution of power, might well produce insurrection and bloodshed on a large scale. He realised that the brutal suppression of colonial peoples would seriously damage Britain's standing and credibility in the eyes of the world. Aware that charges of imperialism and racism were weapons in the Cold War, Macmillan had no wish to alienate Third World opinion. He also feared the spread of communism and the possibility of Africa becoming the new battleground between East and West. In 1960 large scale Russian intervention in Africa seemed imminent as Soviet military personnel were sent to exploit the situation in the Congo. Macmillan, anxious to win the support of the newly emerging Third World countries, thought the best way to do so was to hand over power to local (pro-Western) nationalists.

Macmillan also recognised that British public opinion, indifferent at best to Empire, was unlikely to support substantial new military burdens, particularly if this meant the reintroduction of National Service. Moreover, systematic repression in the colonies was likely to be viewed just as unfavourably at home as abroad. The British government had been embarrassed enough in 1959 by the revelations of maltreatment of Mau Mau detainees at Hola Camp in Kenya. The Labour Party was increasingly sympathetic to African nationalism and critical of white colonial rule.

Perhaps most important of all was the fact that Macmillan, like many policy-makers, could see no good strategic or economic reasons for spending vast sums of money and risking the loss of thousands of lives trying to maintain British rule over people who had no wish to be ruled by Britain. Bitter experience in Palestine, Egypt, Kenya and Cyprus may have helped to weaken Britain's resolve to hang on to her Empire.

Thus by 1960 Macmillan and most of his Cabinet accepted that a fairly rapid withdrawal from Empire was likely to be less painful for all concerned than a long campaign to try to retain control of possessions that would eventually be lost anyway. Macmillan's desire was to construct democratic regimes, well disposed to Britain. He hoped that the new states would remain part of the Commonwealth which would still pivot on the economic and military power of Britain.

The prospect of a rapid transfer of power into the hands of black Africans brought a strong reaction from certain sections of the Conservative Party where the white settler lobby was strong. But Macmillan encountered far less resistance than might have been expected. Many Conservatives accepted Britain's changing interests and realised that it was easier to be swept along by the wind of change than to stand against it. Right-wing Conservatives like Lord Salisbury who did oppose Macmillan's actions found there was relatively little they could do. They were easily isolated because, in the last resort, the Prime Minister could be sure of Labour support for his decolonisation policies.

c) Decolonisation in Africa, 1960-3

The transfer of power was comparatively easy in West Africa where there were few white settlers to complicate the process. In March 1957 the Gold Coast gained its independence and renamed itself Ghana with Nkrumah as President. This was an important step. If the people of Ghana could rule themselves, why not other Africans? Moreover President Nkrumah immediately encouraged independence movements elsewhere in West Africa. In 1960 Nigeria became independent and Sierra Leone followed suite in 1961.

In East Africa Britain had once had hopes of establishing a Federation which would include Tanganyika, Uganda and Kenya, and which would be largely controlled, at least at first, by the white minority in Kenya. (There were very few white settlers in Tanganyika or Uganda.) However, by the late 1950s developments in the three territories convinced British policy-makers that the idea of an East African Federation was a non-starter.

By 1959 it was clear that the Tanganyikan African National Union, led by Julius Nyerere, enjoyed overwhelming African support. Nyerere demanded self-government and threatened strikes and boycotts. Aware that Tanganyika had little economic or strategic importance, Britain promised full independence to Nyerere by December 1961. This set a precedent for the rest of British East Africa.

In 1959 there had seemed little likelihood of Uganda being granted early independence. There were serious tribal divisions within the colony and the possibility of a bloodbath if Britain withdrew too rapidly. However, given the tribal differences, Uganda seemed on the verge of becoming ungovernable or governable only by repression. Britain decided that the best course was to pull out as rapidly and as gracefully as possible. In October 1962 Uganda was given full independence.

Kenya was the most valuable of Britain's East African possessions. The 50,000 white population controlled most of the best land and dominated the Kenyan legislative council, blocking African political advancement. In 1959 there seemed little prospect of either majority rule or independence for Kenya. Jomo Kenyatta, the suspected Mau Mau leader, who had been arrested in 1953, was still in prison and Kenyan whites were certain to oppose anything that could be seen as a 'sell-out' to African nationalism. However, British officials were aware that developments in Tanganyika and Uganda could not be ignored in the most advanced part of British East Africa. Moreover the Kenyan whites were far from united. Some, especially those who were in the British government service (as opposed to those who were farmers), were prepared to break the mould of Kenyan politics and form a multi-racial party. British policy-makers were able to capitalise on this. At a conference in London in January 1960, attended by white and black Kenyan politicians, the ban on African political movements was lifted and a constitution was devised which gave elected Africans a majority in the Kenyan legislature. Once the principle of self-government under majority rule was established, the process towards full democracy and full independence proved impossible to stop. By December 1963 what had seemed unthinkable three years earlier had happened and Kenya had become fully independent under the premiership of Kenyatta.

In Central Africa the end of colonial rule was far more difficult. Britain controlled Northern Rhodesia (with 70,000 whites and 2,000,000 Africans), Nyasaland (7,000 whites and 2,500,000 Africans) and Southern Rhodesia (220,000 whites and 3,500,000 Africans). Britain's control of these territories was complicated by their membership of the Central African Federation, which was dominated by the Southern Rhodesian white settlers. Virtually no steps had been taken to give the Africans any form of political representation. Macmillan's government in 1957 was firmly committed to the idea of the Federation, even though most black Africans were bitterly opposed to it. The British government hoped that white domination would gradually be offset by greater African representation. Nevertheless, in 1957, the prospect of black majority rule seemed remote.

However, in 1959 politics in Central Africa, relatively peaceful since the Federation was established in 1953, became increasingly troubled. Worried by growing disorder and growing support for the African leaders Dr Hastings Banda (in Nyasaland) and Kenneth Kaunda (in Northern Rhodesia), white politicians determined on tough action. In Nyasaland in March 1959 the colonial government, stating they had found evidence of a planned African coup, declared a state of emergency and in the police and military operations which followed 51 Africans were killed. This action proved to be counter-productive. An independent inquiry, headed by Lord Devlin, condemned the Nyasaland government's actions and accused it of running a 'police state'. No previous British colonial government had been so savagely criticised by an official enquiry. After the Devlin Report Britain was reluctant to support more repressive policies.

The main difficulty confronting Britain and white politicians in the Federation after 1959 was the sheer strength and scale of African nationalism in Nyasaland and Northern Rhodesia. Opposition to the white-dominated Federation united virtually all black Africans. As rioting and violence in Nyasaland continued, the danger of a breakdown of authority on a grand scale loomed large. In July 1960 Nyasaland was finally given a constitution which ensured an African majority on its legislative council.

Meanwhile Macmillan had set up a Royal Commission, headed by Walter Monckton, to advise upon the future of the Federation. The Commission reported in October 1960. It concluded that while the Federation was of real economic benefit, African distrust had reached 'almost pathological' proportions and consequently sweeping changes in the structure of the Federation were necessary. It recommended that more power should be devolved to the territories and parity of representation for whites and blacks should be introduced immediately into the Federation's assembly.

Macmillan's government, which basically supported the Monckton's Commission's findings, made great efforts to persuade the Rhodesian whites to make some effort to reach agreement with African leaders. In line with this policy, Macleod announced the creation of a conference to discuss the constitution of Northern Rhodesia.

Sir Roy Welensky, Prime Minister of the Federation, with the support of most Rhodesian whites who were aware of the chaos in the ex-Belgian Congo, was determined to fight what was (correctly) perceived to be a move towards black majority rule in Northern Rhodesia. Complex and bitter negotiations on the future of Northern Rhodesia followed. Hopes of finding a formula for a genuine multi-racial state foundered on the intransigence of both white and black African politicians. Fearing racial conflict, Macmillan was not sure whether to back the white settlers or to support African majority rule. To appease right-wing Conservative pressure, he moved Macleod from the Colonial Office. However, this made little difference. In March 1962 the British Cabinet, convinced that the move to increased African representation was irresistible, accepted majority rule in Northern Rhodesia.

The British government hoped that the granting of African majority rule in Northern Rhodesia and Nyasaland would end the objections to the Federation. Instead, however, black African leaders were now in a much stronger position to campaign for independence from the Federation. In October 1962 elections in Northern Rhodesia (under the new constitution) resulted in victory for African parties, the two largest of which were ready to unite to demand secession. (Nyasaland had already asked to leave the Federation.) It was clear that the Central

African Federation's days were numbered. R.A. Butler, Macmillan's chief lieutenant, presided over the final negotiations which began at the Victoria Falls in June 1963. The Victoria Falls Conference agreed that the Central African Federation should be formally dissolved on 31 December 1963 and that Nyasaland (or Malawi) and Northern Rhodesia (now Zambia) should be given full independence. The collapse of the Federation ended the British dream of multi-racial rule. It also brought with it a further problem - that of Southern Rhodesia where whites refused to concede black majority rule. In December 1962 the Rhodesian Front Party, campaigning on a platform of independence for a white-dominated Southern Rhodesia, won power. Macmillan's government was divided on whether to give Southern Rhodesia independence. Some Conservatives supported white rule which they thought would be more efficient than black African rule. Others, concerned about the future of the majority African population, were opposed to giving independence to a white minority government. Southern Rhodesia, Britain's last foothold in Africa, was to cause problems for the next sixteen years.

White South Africans, like white Rhodesians, were determined to resist the 'wind of change' sweeping through the Africa. Throughout the 1950s the Nationalist government had steadily tightened apartheid, reserving economic and political power for whites. In March 1960 67 Africans, campaigning to get rid of South Africa's oppressive pass laws, were killed in clashes with police at Sharpeville. World-wide condemnation followed. In a 1960 referendum, South African whites voted to make South Africa a republic. Given the change of status, the country had to formally apply to remain in the Commonwealth. Macmillan, seeing no way in which the lot of black South Africans could be improved as a result of South Africa's expulsion from the Commonwealth, supported her continued membership. However, some African and Asian states threatened to leave if South Africa remained in the Commonwealth. South Africa's leader Dr Verwoerd prevented a full-scale crisis by withdrawing his country's application. Even though she was no longer a member of the Commonwealth, Britain continued to have close economic and military ties with South Africa.

d) The West Indies, the Mediterranean and 'East of Suez'

Britain also decolonised in other areas. In the West Indies Britain's main concern was to try to ensure that the new units of government were economically and politically viable. In 1958 she persuaded the dozen or so West Indies colonies to form the West Indian Federation. However, local jealousies and the problems of distance conspired to make the Federation unworkable. In 1962 Jamaica and Trinidad both decided to leave and the Federation collapsed. The larger islands became independent: the smaller islands became Associated States with Britain retaining responsibility for their diplomacy and defence.

Britain also retreated from Cyprus. As opposition to British rule mounted, Macmillan decided that the island was not worth fighting for and opened new talks with Archbishop Makarios, the leader of the Greek Cypriots. After prolonged negotiations an agreement was finally hammered out. Cyprus was to become independent within the Commonwealth in 1960. Its Greek and Turkish communities were each to have almost complete autonomy while Britain retained sovereignty over two bases. It seemed a masterly solution, but trouble between Greek and Turkish Cypriots continued, reaching civil war proportions by 1963.

Malta, once a vital naval base, lost its importance as Britain's naval presence in the Mediterranean decreased. Plans to make Malta an actual part of the United Kingdom collapsed because Britain was unwilling to give the island sufficient financial assistance to bring up the standard of Maltese welfare to that of Britain. Instead, many Maltese demanded independence which was finally granted in September 1964.

Ironically, the retreat from Africa, the West Indies and the Mediterranean, coincided with a new effort to maintain British influence 'east of Suez'. It was feared that if Britain abandoned her role in the Middle and Far East there would be increased instability and a possible communist threat.

In 1957 the Federation of Malaya became independent but Britain assumed responsibility for its defence. By 1961, fearful of growing communist influence in South-East Asia, Britain supported the idea of a Federation of Malaysia which would include Malaya, Singapore and the three remaining British colonies of North Borneo, Brunei and Sarawak. Britain agreed to continue the defence commitments made in 1957. In September 1963 the Federation was officially set up. Indonesia, which had hoped to annex North Borneo and Sarawak, opposed the Federation and for the next three years tried to bring about its disintegration. Britain provided Malaysia with vital military assistance to thwart Indonesian aggression.

Macmillan was also determined to protect Britain's oil interests in the Persian Gulf. Fifty per cent of Britain's oil came from Kuwait, independent since 1961 but still linked to Britain by a defence treaty. In 1961 a British task-force was sent to Kuwait to defend the kingdom against a threatened Iraqi takeover. The move was successful and Iraq quickly backed down.

In the late 1950s Aden, a useful 'springboard' for defending British interests in the Middle East and the Indian Ocean, became a major British base. However the colony was threatened by Arab nationalism both from without (especially from neighbouring Yemen) and from within Aden itself. To try to provide some support for Aden, Britain created a new South Arabian Federation in 1963 - a collection of undemocratic, semi-feudal sheikdoms on the south coast of the Arabian peninsula. This did not solve matters and terrorism in Aden increased. But Britain seemed determined to retain the base and was prepared to repress all opposition.

An average of 100,000 British service personnel were based east of Suez after 1960 and a Chiefs of Staff planning study in 1962 envisaged a major role for Britain in the Indian Ocean for at least the next decade. British policy east of Suez, supported by most Conservative and many Labour MPs, shows that the concept of a global British role had still not been abandoned.

e) Decolonisation: Conclusion

In the early 1960s colonial rule almost everywhere came to an end far more quickly and far less satisfactorily than the British government intended. The idea that some colonies were unprepared, too poor or too small to become independent was tacitly abandoned. Most whites in Africa believed that Macmillan had caved in far too easily to African nationalist pressure. Most historians, however, are of the opinion that Britain divested herself of Empire with some dignity and skill. There was remarkably little bloodshed abroad and no major political crisis in Britain. The British public, reassured from all sides that Britain would remain a world power, watched the process of disintegration with indifference. It was generally assumed that formal Empire would be replaced by informal influence, sealed by economic ties and defence treaties.

6 The European Common Market

Since 1945 all British governments had been reluctant to embroil Britain in European efforts at co-operation. It was not surprising then that Britain did not join Germany, France, Italy, Holland, Belgium and Luxemburg and sign the Treaty of Rome in March 1957 which established the European Economic Community (EEC), popularly known as the Common Market. The three main aims of the EEC were the removal of all internal tariffs, the free movement of labour and capital within the community, and the adoption of a common external tariff to be imposed on goods entering the Community. The Treaty of Rome also defined the institutions which would be responsible for the Community - the Council of Ministers, the European Commission, the European Assembly, and the Court of Justice.

In 1957 Macmillan's government expressed no wish to join the EEC. It was widely feared that a common external tariff would seriously damage Britain's special trade relationship with the Empire/Commonwealth and the latter, with its population of over 800 million, seemed a more promising market than the EEC which had under 200 million.

Macmillan, like most British policymakers, also disliked the supra-national implications of the Common Market which seemed to threaten national sovereignty. Britain, therefore, 'missed out' in Europe at a time when the British government might have decisively influenced the EEC's rules and structure, and when it might have been possible to negotiate reasonable deals for British agriculture and for the Empire/Commonwealth.

Worried about being excluded from trade with the EEC, Britain now tried to create a counter-balance with countries that felt similarly threatened. In January 1960, Britain, in collaboration with Norway, Denmark, Sweden, Austria, Portugal and Switzerland, established the European Free Trade Association (EFTA). This contained no supra-national institutions and the free trade area did not apply to agricultural products.

Yet within two years of joining EFTA Britain applied to join the EEC. Historians have different views about the main reasons for this change of policy. Some stress the importance of economic factors. By the late 1950s it was evident that the EEC was an outstanding economic success and that the British economy was lagging significantly behind that of its European competitors. By 1961 Britain had, in Macmillan's view, 'terrifying' economic problems. Her share of the world's manufacturing exports was steadily declining and she had a growing trade deficit. There was also a shift in the focus of Britain's trading activity away from Empire/Commonwealth and towards Western Europe. The Common-wealth, in spite of its size, could not compare with the purchasing power of the EEC. Britain, it seemed, needed the large tariff free market offered by the EEC to prevent her economy going into steep decline.

In public, Macmillan laid great stress on the supposed economic advantages of membership of the EEC. However, many historians now think that international considerations played a more significant role. Macmillan feared that a powerful EEC would replace Britain as the European pillar of the Atlantic alliance and thus endanger Britain's special relationship with the USA. The fact that the USA, anxious to see Britain pursuing primarily a European role in world affairs, encouraged Britain to join the EEC may also have carried some weight. Macmillan believed that membership of the EEC would help maintain and possibly enhance British influence both within Europe and with the USA. He was confident that once inside the EEC Britain could take over the leadership.

By 1960 Macmillan was convinced that it was in Britain's best interest to join the EEC but before he could begin formal negotiations, he had to convince his Cabinet, Parliament, the Conservative Party, the country and the Commonwealth. Opposition within the Cabinet was slowly weeded out as Macmillan reshuffled his ministry putting pro-Europeans, like Edward Heath, into key positions. By December 1960 Macmillan had convinced most of his Cabinet colleagues of the need for EEC entry and ministers were sent to discover the reaction of Britain's Commonwealth partners. In Britain important sections of the press, banking and industry were positive and public opinion did not seem hostile. In July 1961, therefore, Macmillan told the Commons that the government wished to join the EEC, provided that British, Commonwealth and EFTA interests could all be safeguarded. In the subsequent debate the government gained a comfortable majority of over 100 for its initiative.

In October 1961 negotiations aimed at securing Britain's entry into the EEC began. Edward Heath, leader of the British delegation, spoke of Britain's desire, 'to become a full, whole-hearted and active member of the European Community in the widest sense'. The rest of 1961 and the whole of 1962 were taken up with detailed negotiations. It was soon clear that there were major stumbling blocks, particularly in relation to British agriculture, and also Britain's concern to protect the interests of Commonwealth countries, especially Australia and New Zealand, both of which could be damaged by the EEC's Common Agricultural Policy.

There remained also the tricky question of sovereignty. In a television interview in September 1962, the Labour leader Hugh Gaitskell warned that if Britain joined the EEC, 'we become no more than Texas or California in the United States of Europe. It means the end of a thousand years of History'. Gaitskell was in tune with many in the Labour Party who feared the loss of British independence and the damage British EEC membership would do to the Commonwealth. But Edward Heath pressed forward with the negotiations, convinced that European unity was essential and that entry to the EEC was in Britain's best interests.

However, by the autumn of 1962, it was clear that there were powerful European adversaries to Britain's admission. Konrad Adenauer, the West German Chancellor, did not like or trust Macmillan and suspected that Britain was applying for EEC membership mainly with the intent of trying to undermine French-German unity. Germany, however, was not the main problem. Almost certainly, acceptable terms could have been agreed between Britain and the EEC but for General de Gaulle.

Historians still debate precisely why the French leader was opposed to British entry in 1962-3. One underlying problem was that de Gaulle had a deep-seated American-British phobia dating from the Second World War. He also felt that Britain was too entangled with both the Commonwealth and the USA to readily become a 'good' European power. The French President was concerned that Britain might be an American Trojan horse, bringing unwelcome American influence into Europe. The strongly nationalistic de Gaulle also regarded the EEC as an instrument of renewed French hegemony in Europe and feared that Britain might be an inconvenient rival to French supremacy.

Many historians see the Kennedy-Macmillan Polaris agreement of

December 1962 as the final straw as far as de Gaulle was concerned. Rather than co-operate with France in nuclear matters, it seemed that Britain preferred to be tied to the USA. If the Polaris agreement caused the French leader to genuinely change his view of the desirability of Britain's membership of the EEC, the Polaris deal can be viewed as a mistake on Macmillan's part. Alternatively, however, (and on balance this seems more likely), Polaris may just have been the excuse that de Gaulle was looking for in order to prevent Britain's entry into the EEC. If this is the case, and if British Intelligence had made it clear that a French veto was almost certain, the Polaris agreement and the haggling in favour of Commonwealth exports no longer appear to have been tactical errors.

Last minute talks between Macmillan and de Gaulle in December 1962 achieved nothing. On 14 January 1963 de Gaulle announced his opposition to British entry and French representatives at the Council of Ministers imposed a veto on further negotiations. The fact that all the other EEC members, in principle, welcomed Britain's admission made no difference.

At the time the French veto was not generally seen as a national defeat largely because the EEC was not yet regarded as a cure for all Britain's ills. Many, on both right and left, were delighted that Britain's attempt to join the EEC had failed. Few blamed Macmillan for the failure. Most historians, like most contemporaries, blame de Gaulle and think it unlikely that anything anyone could have done would have had much effect.

However, Macmillan was devastated by the French veto. He had come to see British membership of the EEC as an essential part of his strategy for reviving Britain. The Prime Minister wrote in his diary on 28 January 1963, 'All our policies at home and abroad are in ruins'.

7 The End of Macmillan

On the eve of the Conservative Party Conference in October 1963 Macmillan was struck by illness (an inflamed prostate gland) and on doctor's orders announced his resignation - a move he regretted after his speedy recovery from the operation. He was replaced by Lord Home (pronounced Hume) who chose to renounce his peerage and became plain Sir Alexander Douglas-Home. 'Sir Alec' had entered the Cabinet as Secretary of State for Commonwealth Relations in 1957 and become Foreign Secretary in 1960.

Home was Prime Minister for one - difficult - year. In Europe he had to try to pick up the pieces left by the French veto of Britain's EEC application. Following President Kennedy's assassination in November 1966, Anglo-American relations were less cordial. Home failed to establish a close relationship with President Johnson: the two men were very different in style, method and temperament; and the USA found itself increasingly involved in Vietnam, a country in which Britain had little interest.

In the run up to the 1964 general election it seemed that there were no great Conservative and Labour divisions on foreign matters. The new Labour leader Harold Wilson was committed to Britain retaining a nuclear deterrent and remaining in NATO. Both Wilson and Home supported maintaining the special relationship with the USA. Both accepted that there was no immediate possibility of entering the EEC. Both still expressed hope in the future of a British-led Commonwealth and both believed Britain had an important role to play east of Suez. It did not seem, therefore, that Labour's narrow success in the 1964 election would make much difference to British external affairs.

8 Macmillan: conclusion

It is difficult to decide whether Macmillan's successes in foreign and imperial affairs outweighed his failures. His critics have accused him of constant U-turns, of kow-towing to the USA, of surrendering the British Empire too quickly, of trying - and failing - to enter the EEC, and of failing to find Britain a viable world role. His supporters on the other hand, can point to a number of successes - his special relationship with Presidents Eisenhower and Kennedy, his efforts to ease East-West tension culminating in the 1963 Test Ban Treaty, the skilful and relatively painless withdrawal from Africa, and (despite the 1963 French veto) his pointing the way for Britain's ultimate entry to the EEC.

However, in the final analysis, Macmillan had been unable to square the circles - to preserve Britain's links with the USA, to strengthen her Commonwealth links, and at the same time maintain a leading role in Europe by bringing Britain within the EEC. By 1963 Churchill's notion that Britain might continue to exert real world power because of her relations with the USA, the Commonwealth and Europe, was probably unrealistic. A small island with a declining economic base could not play a pivotal world role in the age of the superpowers. Retreat and re-direction had to be the order of the day. Macmillan had the good sense to realise this. He retreated - and tried to redirect British policy - and he did so with not a little skill and with considerable panache. Macmillan said that his philosophy of life is, 'there are neither successes or failures, you do your best and that's my life'. This might be a suitable epitaph to his external policy-making.

Making notes on '*The Wind of Change, 1957-64*'
Your notes on this chapter should help you to answer the following questions:
1. How strong was the 'special relationship' 1957-64?

Year	Relations with USSR	Relations with USA	Defence Policy	Relations with Europe	Empire/Commonwealth
1957	Khruschev				Africa
1958	Berlin	Eisenhower	Defence White Paper	Treaty of Rome	
1959			Skybolt		Slow Decolonisation
1960			End of Conscription	EFTA	Rapid Decolonisation (Why?)
1961		Kennedy		EEC Application	
1962	Cuba Crisis		Polaris		Middle East / Far East — USA involvement
1963	Test Ban Treaty			French Veto	'East of Suez' Role

Summary – The Wind of Change, 1957-64

2. Why did Britain decolonise so speedily 1957-64?
3. Why did Britain apply for membership of the EEC and why did that application fail?
4. How successful was Macmillan in foreign and imperial matters? As you read the chapter try to identify why Macmillan acted as he did. What could he have done that was different? It is also worth studying the maps on page 22 and page 130 so that you are familiar with the countries and areas mentioned in the text.

Answering essay questions on 'The Wind of Change, 1957-64'

Questions on British foreign and imperial policy in the period 1957-64 are likely to fall into the four categories highlighted in the 'notes' section: relations with the USA (and the USSR); decolonisation; EEC application; and general overview. Here are some examples:

  1 To what extent was Macmillan's 'special relationship' with the USA of benefit to Britain?
  2 'Macmillan surrendered to the forces of African nationalism'. Discuss this statement.
  3 Account for Britain's decision to apply for membership of the EEC in 1961 and for the failure of Britain's application.
  4 'His successes outweighed his failures'. Discuss this verdict on Macmillan's foreign and imperial policies.

While covering the same chronological period, these titles require very different emphasis. Consider each of the titles in turn. Try a 'brain-storming' session to pinpoint the various arguments you could put forward, and then go on to establish which ones you could argue effectively. When you have sorted out your views, try to work out a paragraph-by-paragraph plan for each title.

Question 1 asks you to focus on Macmillan's relationship with the USA. The danger is that you will write all you know about Macmillan's relationship with Eisenhower and Kennedy. Unfortunately that is not what this particular question asks! What you need to do is decide whether Britain gained or lost from the 'special relationship' in the period 1957-63. What would your conclusion be?

Question 2 is easier. You will need to decide whether you basically agree with the quote or not. Remember there is no right or wrong answer. It is up to you to assemble your evidence to support whatever argument you decide to adopt. You should, however, indicate that you are aware that there are many different explanations for Britain's decision to decolonise so quickly. If you disagree with the quote you will probably point out that it is at best over-simplistic! You should then go on to examine the various factors which prompted decolonisation. If you think that African nationalism was a major factor in Britain's decision to decolonise so quickly, you should still indicate that other factors were at work as well.

A list of reasons for British application for EEC membership and for why that application failed will go some way to answering question 3. But how will you frame your essay so as to avoid it appearing like a list? What overall argument will you give?

The main difficulty with question 4 might be deciding what to include and what to miss out. Construct both an introduction and a conclusion for this question. Remember to highlight what you consider to be Macmillan's main successes and failures. Do you agree or disagree with the quote?

Source-based questions on 'The Wind of Change, 1957-64'

1 The 1957 Defence White Paper
Read the extract from the 1957 Defence White Paper on pages 121-2. Answer the following questions:
a) What obligations did Britain have to NATO? (2 marks)
b) What did the White Paper mean when it spoke of Britain's 'special responsibilities in many parts of the world'? (3 marks)
c) Comment on the statement, 'The Communist threat remains, but its nature has changed'. (4 marks)
d) What did the White Paper see as the main economic reasons for a change of policy? (4 marks)
e) What arguments might opponents of the White Paper have raised? (7 marks)

2 Decolonisation
Read the extract from the 1957 Cabinet Colonial Policy Committee on page 126 and the extract from Macmillan's 1960 speech in South Africa on page 128. Answer the following questions:
a) In what way do the two extracts differ? (4 marks)
b) What did Macmillan mean when he spoke of 'fifteen years ago this movement spread through Asia'? (3 marks)
c) What did he mean by the 'wind of change'? (3 marks)
d) How significant was the fact that Macmillan delivered the 1960 speech in South Africa? (5 marks)

CHAPTER 8

External Affairs 1939-64: A Conclusion

In November 1964 the Labour Prime Minister Harold Wilson declared, 'We are a world power and a world influence or we are nothing'. In 1965 he stated that as far as he was concerned Britain remained a world power whose frontiers 'are on the Himalayas'. However, whatever Wilson might say, it was clear to everyone that Britain was no longer a first rate world power. By 1964 the British Empire had virtually gone. Eclipsed by the USA and the USSR, Britain was no longer one of the 'managers' in world politics. Why had Britain declined so much in the period 1939-64? Who or what was to blame?

1 Was Britain's Decline Inevitable?

There seems little doubt that Britain's decline was always possible and perhaps probable. Britain's Empire, on which her greatness largely depended, was never as strong as it appeared on the map. By the early twentieth century it was clear that Britain lacked both the will and the means to make much of her Empire. It was almost inevitable that sooner or later colonial subjects would grow restless and demand greater freedom. The theory behind British colonisation had always been that British rule was a preparation for home rule. By 1931 the 'white' dominions were fully independent and by 1939 India was on the verge of being granted dominion status. It was always unlikely that a nation with only 2 per cent of the world's population could continue to control over 20 per cent of its land surface.

Britain's imperial power was to a large extent dependent on her economic position. By the late-nineteenth century, however, Britain's dominant economic position was under threat (especially from the USA and Germany) and Britain's share of the world's wealth began to diminish. This had implications for Britain's ability to sustain military commitments around the world. Moreover, as aircraft and submarines developed, Britain's naval supremacy, which had ensured her security at home and dominance abroad, was no longer enough.

However, Britain's weakness before the Second World War should not be exaggerated. In 1939 Britain conducted as much international trade as the USA. Britain's industrial economy, while much smaller than the USA's, was comparable with Germany's and much stronger than Japan's. Ramshackle, multi-ethnic empires can survive for long periods, as the Ottoman and Habsburg Empires proved in the nineteenth century, if their rulers have the will to survive. Pre-1939 British governments had that will. Britain found it relatively easy to contain colonial nationalism by working with collaborators who could see benefits of close association with Britain, and by displaying military power in an emergency. The dominions continued to be British satellites.

It seems reasonable to conclude, therefore, that but for the Second World War, Britain might well have retained her great power status far longer than was to be the case. In international politics appearances of power are often as important as actual substance. Nor was British power just 'appearance'. Britain was a hard nut to crack as the Second World War was to prove.

2 The Effect of the Second World War

The Second World War was a vital factor in Britain's decline. Britain went to war in 1939, according to the historian John Charmley, 'in a spasm of self-righteousness indignation, convinced that as a great power, it was her duty to defeat Nazi Germany'. She was allied only with Poland and France. Poland was quickly defeated and the events of 1940 exposed Anglo-French military weaknesses. By July 1940 Britain appeared to have little option but to sign a humiliating truce with Hitler or face catastrophic defeat. However, by a combination of stubbornness and good fortune, Britain's bacon was saved, first by Hitler's attack on the USSR, and then by the entry of the USA into the war.

In order to defeat Germany (and Italy and Japan) Britain was reliant on the economic strength of the USA and the manpower of the USSR. British industry and military strength by itself was not sufficient. Although Britain's manpower losses were less severe than those sustained in the First World War, the economic cost of the Second World War was greater. American firms were required to provide essential war material that Britain could not produce. In consequence there was a horrendous drain on Britain's holdings of gold and dollars. On top of this Britain lost vital export markets and was forced to sell a large proportion of her overseas assets. By 1945 Britain had lost a quarter of her pre-war wealth and had become the world's largest debtor nation. The British economist Keynes admitted that during the war, 'We threw good housekeeping to the winds'. The war, therefore, left Britain in a terribly weakened economic position and very much dependent on the USA which had very different economic interests to Britain, particularly with regard to imperial preference.

Although the Second World War left Britain much stronger than Germany and Japan (and France!), Britain could no longer compare in strength with the USA and the USSR. As Churchill lamented, compared with the 'huge Russian bear' and the 'great American elephant', the British lion seemed small indeed. Churchill had failed (before 1939) to realise that this was always a likely outcome of the Second World War. Despite Britain's (in many ways glorious) role in the defeat of Hitler, it can be claimed that it was a mistake to get involved in war with Germany in September 1939. As Chamberlain had recognised, Britain had nothing to gain and everything to lose from a war, even a successful one. Britain had gone to war to prevent Hitler dominating East and Central Europe. By 1945 the same area was dominated by Stalin, in many ways as ruthless and threatening as Hitler. By 1945 Churchill was aware that the prospect of winning the war but losing the peace was a very real one.

The war then saw a shift in the global balance of power away from Western Europe and towards the USA and the USSR. The Age of the Superpower had arrived. After 1945 Britain was always likely to find herself dwarfed by the sheer scale of American and Soviet economic power and resources. It was also likely that she would find it increasingly difficult to hold together her scattered Empire that was ideologically offensive and a practical inconvenience to both the USA and the USSR.

Yet arguably Britain's position in 1945 was not impossible. She retained her Empire. She was one of the Big Three. She possessed great military resources. Many politicians thought it would only be a matter of time before she recovered her economic strength. Some historians, therefore, place the blame for Britain's decline fairly and squarely on post-war British governments and/or specific policy-makers. Other historians, however, are quite prepared to defend the record of the various governments/statesmen! The next two sections will set out the main arguments against - and then for - the governments.

3 The Case Against British Governments, 1945-64

Different historians have targeted different governments - and different statesman - for blame. But some condemn a whole generation of British policy-makers for pursuing inconsistent and directionless policies, invariably citing the words of former American Secretary of State, Dean Acheson, in 1962: 'Great Britain has lost an empire and has not yet found a role'.

One of the main charges against all British governments after 1945 is that they continued to cherish the illusion that Britain could somehow remain a great power. The result was that an exhausted Britain continued to have unprecedented military commitments both in Europe and around the world. High defence spending weakened Britain's fragile economy. Scarce resources of manpower and raw materials, could have been better employed modernising Britain's industry. In consequence, it is claimed, Britain lost her industrial competitiveness. In 1950 Britain generated 25 per cent of the total value of the world's manufactured exports. By 1960 this had slumped to 16 per cent.

Many left-wing historians and politicians have been particularly critical of post-war governments for supporting the production of Britain's own nuclear bombs and for purchasing American missile systems. They have questioned the need for a (so-called) independent nuclear deterrent, claiming that this was terribly expensive, encouraged the proliferation of nuclear weapons and, far from deterring, possibly actually encouraged a Soviet nuclear attack on Britain.

Other critics have attacked the post-war governments for being too pro-USA with the result that Britain became little more than an American satellite. They have questioned the need for the special relationship, arguing that the Soviet threat was greatly exaggerated. The Russians, it is claimed, were already seriously over-extended and were more concerned with defence than with expanding communist influence. Even if there was a Soviet threat, many have pointed out that the special relationship meant little given that the USA was so much stronger than Britain. Britain, for example, had no real control over American policy at the time of the Cuban Missiles Crisis in 1962, a crisis which threatened Britain with destruction. Moreover, British and American interests were far from identical and the USA did not always prove herself a particularly good ally as the 1956 Suez crisis showed only too clearly.

However, Britain cannot blame the USA for the loss of its Empire. Although most Americans disliked colonial empires, by the late 1940s the USA recognised the value of British support against the USSR and realised the importance of the British Empire in the Cold War struggle. In fact, neither superpower showed much interest in penetrating the regions in which British interests were concentrated. The emergence of the two superpowers, therefore, did not in itself, lead to the end of the British imperial system. Consequently post-war British governments shoulder much of the blame for the loss of the Empire.

Colonial rule, almost everywhere, came to an end far more quickly and far less satisfactorily than most British policy-makers intended - often with terrible results for the ex-colonial territories. The transfer of authority was too swift to allow democratic constitutions to strike deep roots. The result was that the parliamentary democracies which Britain left behind soon withered and died. Attlee's government has been particularly criticised for the way it abandoned India. Some think the sub-continent could and should have been held by resolute action. Others think better management could have prevented the bloodbath which followed Britain's withdrawal. Many historians have blamed Eden for Suez. This is often seen as a major turning point in British external affairs. Until 1956 Britain can be seen as 'holding the line'. After Suez Britain could no longer conceal her impotence and the rush of colonial territories for independence became a flood. Macmillan can also be criticised for giving up Britain's African colonies too quickly.

Arguably the threat from colonial nationalism was greatly exaggerated. Britain, given the tremendous divisions within most colonial territories, could easily have found reliable collaborators who feared the coming to power of a rival tribe, community or religious group. Dividing the opposition and winning new friends was the oldest routine in the colonial act. Rarely, even at the point of independence, were colonial politicians sufficiently united to worry Britain unduly. In many colonies there was little enthusiasm for a real struggle against British rule and in some there was a positive desire that it should remain. Most British statesmen deluded themselves into believing that by granting independence so easily they would win the co-operation of local political leaders and that the new states would remain part of a New Commonwealth which would continue to be dominated by Britain. However, from the start the notion of the New Commonwealth was fuzzy. The various new states, unlike the old 'white' dominions, had little in common in religious, racial, political and economic terms. Sentimental ties alone, even ties of kith and kin, were never likely to provide strong links without a solid material base and after 1945 Britain could not offer enough reward for association in the form of trade, investment and military protection. Given the lack of common interests, it should have been clear from the start that the idea of the Commonwealth as the vehicle through which British influence could continue to be maintained was simply a pipedream.

Arguably Britain's fixation with the English-speaking world blinded her to the significance of moves for European integration until it was too late. British governments, of both parties, can be blamed for not enthusiastically taking the lead in Western Europe after 1945. The result was that Britain missed joining the EEC, an organisation which ensured greater economic growth for its members than Britain managed. Britain's application to join the EEC in 1961-3 was less than enthusiastic. This reluctance, which helped produce the French veto, ensured Britain did not join the EEC until 1973, after its basic shape had been determined.

4 The Case For British Governments, 1945-64

However, British governments and individual statesmen in this period do have their defenders. Sympathetic historians have pointed out the great difficulties facing British policy-makers - economic weakness, changing weapons of war, the rise of the two superpowers, the Soviet threat in Europe, and the challenge from colonial nationalism. It could be that Acheson's view, that Britain had lost an empire and not yet found a role, was mistaken. (Macmillan in his diary said that Acheson was 'always a conceited ass'!) Even now, with the benefit of hindsight, it is difficult to see precisely what role Britain could or should have adopted. Although various historians and politicians have argued that British post-war governments got their priorities wrong, there is still no consensus on what those priorities should have been and no agreement on precisely when the fundamental mistakes were made. Should Britain have tried to uphold its imperial traditions through an evolving Commonwealth? Should it have attempted to strengthen its trans-

Atlantic links? Or was Britain's place really in Europe? All these strategies had and have critics as well as supporters. Perhaps the wisest course was to try to maintain Britain's great power status by operating in all three 'circles'.

British leaders of all parties after 1945 felt it incumbent to maintain Britain's world status. Britain had won the Second World War. If Britain was not a superpower on the scale of the USA and the USSR, a wide gulf separated her from all other powers. In 1945 she had a significant military presence in over 40 countries for the purpose of maintaining order or deterring potential aggressors. If Britain had not fulfilled her obligations chaos might well have ensued to the likely benefit of the USSR. Most policy-makers appreciated that Britain was over-committed and that trying to maintain great power status might sap the power it was supposed to protect. But most politicians argued that rapid withdrawal anywhere could undermine Britain's international prestige and once the prestige of a country has started to slide there is, as Eden noted in 1952, 'no knowing where it will stop'.

In order to hold on to her position and maintain her national security, Britain had no choice but to spend huge sums on defence. A large navy was needed to protect the trade routes and the Empire. A large army was needed as a result of Britain's commitments both in Europe and overseas. The RAF was vital because of the deterrent effect of bombing, enhanced by the development of the V-bomber force in the mid 1950s which carried Britain's nuclear bomb. The fact that Britain had a nuclear deterrent meant that she had the trappings of being a great power. Given that there was no guarantee that America would always wish to defend Europe, the British bomb was an insurance policy against the possibility of a future American withdrawal from NATO. Possibly the building up of the British economy might in the long run have done more for Britain's prestige and position in the world than the atomic bomb. But it is unlikely that Britain's industrial problems would have been solved if the country had not produced the bomb.

It is sometimes forgotten that the post-war governments did have some economic success. British exports quadrupled between 1944 and 1950 and Britain's balance of payments were in equilibrium by 1948. The sale of military hardware to foreign countries, whether morally right or wrong, made an important contribution to Britain's export drive. It is also worth remembering that Conservative governments in the 1950s were successful in reducing Britain's defence spending and managed to abolish national service.

Many historians would praise, rather than blame, successive British governments for establishing good relationships with the USA and for ensuring that the USA committed itself to the defence of Western Europe. Far from being over-dependent on the USA, dependence on the USA was vital. Most historians believe that there was a Soviet threat. Given that Russian plans were kept secret, the Western allies had to infer

Soviet intentions from Soviet actions - and these were menacing. Stalin's refusal to allow free elections in Eastern Europe, despite war-time promises, was an indication of his untrustworthiness. Wherever possible the USSR set up Soviet-style regimes, subservient to Moscow. The costs of being wrong about the Soviet threat were so enormous that arguably Britain had no option but to combine with the USA to deter the USSR from taking military action in Europe.

The notion that Britain might somehow have played the role of honest broker between the two superpowers is a non-starter. The idea that Europe, or the Commonwealth or the United Nations (or somehow all three!) could offer an alternative power base for Britain made little practical sense. In most respects, Britain and the USA were natural allies. Although the special relationship was increasingly unbalanced, it did give Britain unusual access to American policy-makers and yielded important results, not least the nuclear alliance of the late 1950s and early 1960s.

No post-war British government wished to jettison the country's imperial spheres of influence, essential if Britain was to maintain her world power pretensions. Moreover the colonies provided the foodstuffs and raw materials which would otherwise have to be bought with precious dollars. Attlee's government, sometimes blamed for starting the decolonisation process, appreciated the economic value of the Empire. It had little alternative but to quit India and Palestine and did well to do so with so little bloodshed. Although Suez turned out to be a profound miscalculation on Eden's part, it did not change much, at most accelerating the process of the disintegration of British imperial power by a few years. Most historians have defended Harold Macmillan for his colonial policies after 1957. Brutal colonial conflicts were avoided and Britain succeeded in remaining on good terms with most of her former territories.

Britain naturally hoped to give up her imperial burdens but still to enjoy the imperial perks. The belief that Britain could transform an Empire which she ruled into a Commonwealth over which she would have effective influence and which would benefit Britain's economic and strategic interests, seemed a viable proposition in the 1950s. Canada, New Zealand and Australia still had important ties of kinship with Britain which gave the Commonwealth some strength and solidarity. Preference in trade benefitted most Commonwealth countries. Colonial leaders, appeased by the granting of independence and constitutional equality with Britain, might have been prepared to accept a satellite role in a British-led Commonwealth, as dominion Prime Ministers had done before 1945. Unfortunately, after 1945 Britain lacked the military and economic resources that made close association worthwhile. Britain, therefore, ultimately failed to substitute Commonwealth influence for imperial rule but it is understandable why the attempt was made.

It is easy, with hindsight, to claim that the post-war governments missed the European bus. However, in the years immediately after 1945, the European option seemed a distraction from Britain's real interests. Integration with economically weak and politically unstable West European states seemed less attractive than maintaining traditional imperial links. Most statesmen, like most British people, had a weak sense of European identity. In 1952 Eden spoke for many when he said:

1 Our thoughts move across the seas to the many commitments in which our people play their part, in every corner of the world. These are our family ties. That is our life. Without it we should be no more than some millions of people living on an island off the
5 coast of Europe, in which nobody wants to take any particular interest.

Britain was not in a position to take on the role of leadership in Europe because she did not want to go where other European countries would follow her. She had no wish to sacrifice her sovereignty to supra-national agencies. She had no wish to see barriers imposed against trade with the Empire/Commonwealth. However, the progressive integration of post-war Europe and the economic success of the EEC (neither of which had been foreseen in the early 1950s) provided both a challenge and an opportunity for Britain. Hopeful that EEC membership would bring faster economic growth, and fearing that the price of remaining outside the EEC might be a dramatic contraction of British influence in the Western alliance, Macmillan's government decided it had little option but to seek membership of the EEC, even if this placed a question mark over the whole future of the Common-wealth. It is possible to argue that Macmillan's government moved swiftly to repair the damage caused by failing to join the EEC sooner. There was little Macmillan could have done to prevent the French veto in 1963.

5 British Public Opinion

All British governments after 1945 had to respond to British public opinion. In the British political system the influence of public opinion was (and is) indirect. No plebiscites were held on external (or domestic) policy. Nevertheless, opinion was crucially tested in by-elections, general elections and increasingly by opinion polls. Politicians were aware that certain things would or would not be tolerated by the British public. By the late 1950s, for example, there seems to have been a powerful state of indifference (at best!) to Empire. Most Britons, encouraged by a media which was predominantly liberal, humane and moralistic, frowned on old coercive methods of maintaining colonial authority and were less prepared to accept those arguments for maintaining white minority rule which depended upon a blunt assertion of white superiority.

The British public after 1945 was far more concerned with bread and butter issues - the cost of living, employment, education, housing etc - than with maintaining Empire or joining the EEC. This, perhaps, helps explain why, throughout the years of imperial dissolution, there was amazing political stability at home.

6 Conclusion

After 1939 the international conditions, which had allowed Britain and other European states to 'control' so large a part of the earth's surface, altered. This was, in part, the result of the Second World War. But it is likely that the rise of the two superpowers, demands for colonial independence and British economic decline might have occurred with or without the Second World War. The same can be said of changes in military technology - the development of airpower, missiles and nuclear weapons - which negated Britain's geographical advantages of insularity. Britain, a small, densely populated island, was far more vulnerable to nuclear devastation than the USA or the USSR. Given the changing conditions, Britain's decline was always probable.

British statesmen adjusted reasonably well to the realities of the situation. The paramount aim of foreign policy, the maintenance of national security, was achieved. War against Germany may have been a mistake but at least Britain emerged on the victorious side and had seen off (for a generation) the challenge from Germany and Japan. Post-1945 British governments succeeded (with considerable American help) in holding the communist threat at bay without bankrupting the country and with relatively little fighting (Korea apart). The Empire, an increasing embarrassment, was disposed of smoothly and without the bitter experiences of France in Indo-China and Algeria.

Most British Prime Ministers and Foreign Secretaries of this period are praised rather than damned by historians. Churchill, for all his faults, was a great war leader. Attlee and Bevin have more defenders that critics. Churchill and Eden in the early 1950s did reasonably well. Suez was a serious blot on Eden's copybook but lessons were learnt from this traumatic episode. Most historians are positive about Harold Macmillan who built an impressive reputation as an international statesman.

The statesman, however, should not take all the credit. Luck, rather than skill, was often on Britain's side. In the Second World War, the USSR and USA came to her rescue. After the war, the USA came to Europe's defence and Britain was the main beneficiary of American aid.

In 1964 Britain still occupied a role in international affairs out of all proportion to her size and population. She still had substantial commitments east of Suez. British commerce and investment in the world were still extensive. British cultural influence - the English language, the BBC World Service, sport (especially cricket) - were important. The Commonwealth remained a force to be reckoned with, giving Britain a point of contact with many Third World countries. Britain was one of the world's five nuclear powers.

Britain was no longer a superpower in 1964. It should be said, however, that superpowers do not always find life at the top a comfortable or rewarding experience. And although Britain had declined in the period 1939 to 1964, far worse scenarios - the what-might-have-beens - can easily be envisaged. It can even be claimed that after 1945, despite all the problems, the world evolved on lines very much in accord with Britain's true interests - peace and prosperity.

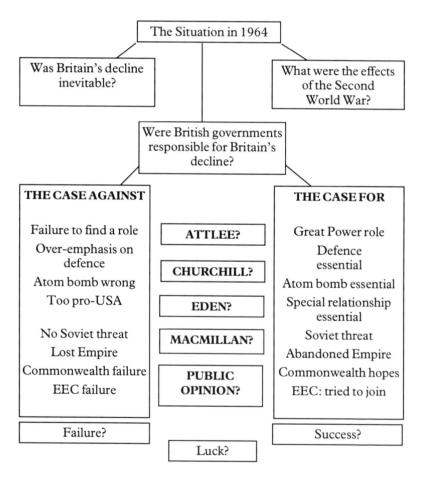

Summary - External Affairs 1939-64: A Conclusion

Working on *'External Affairs 1939-64: A Conclusion'*

This chapter reconsiders many of the issues raised in chapter 1, and in particular, assesses the extent to which British governments and statesmen should be held responsible for the decline in Britain's status. What mistakes did governments make? Which government was most to blame? These are questions which historians (and politicians) still debate. Your notes should set out the extent to which British governments were in a position to control foreign and imperial affairs. What problems did they face? What might have been done differently? Did governments act rationally and in Britain's best interests? Throughout the chapter you have been challenged to formulate your own judgements - and now is the time to do so. You should not necessarily agree with the last section of this chapter which (almost) suggests that things ended happily ever after! What arguments would you put forward to challenge this positive view of British external policy-making?

It is worth while thinking about the following essay title:

Discuss the view that Britain's decline in world power in the period 1939-64 was inevitable.

You should by now have realised the importance of composing first paragraphs for essays and should be able to do so quite quickly. Unfortunately you still have 7 or 8 other paragraphs to write. Make a detailed plan to indicate the main themes of these paragraphs. Finally you must bring the essay to a rational conclusion. What would you write? And now the litmus test of any essay! Imagine an examiner only reads your introduction and conclusion. Does your introduction set the scene? Does your conclusion present a good summary of the rest of the planned essay? Do your introduction and conclusion together go a long way to answering the set question? If not, think of ways you could improve matters. If so, remember to use the successful formula in future essays!

Chronological Table

1939	September	Start of Second World War.
	October	Hitler peace proposals.
	November	Russia invaded Finland.
1940	April	Germany occupied Denmark and Norway.
	May	Chamberlain resigned. Churchill became Prime Minister.
	May	Start of Battle of France.
	May-June	Dunkirk.
	June	Italy entered the war.
	June	France surrendered.
	July	Hitler 'Peace Offensive'
	July-Sept.	Battle of Britain.
	December	Eden became Foreign Secretary.
1941	March	American Lend-Lease to Britain.
	March-April	Germany overran Yugoslavia and Greece.
	June	Germany attacked the USSR.
	August	Atlantic Charter.
	December	Pearl Harbor. The USA entered the war.
1942	February	Fall of Singapore.
	August	Churchill visited Moscow.
	Oct.-Nov.	Battle of El Alamein.
	November	Anglo-American force landed in Morocco.
1943	January	Casablanca meeting.
	January	Germans surrendered at Stalingrad.
	May	Germans surrendered at Tunis.
	July	Allied invasion of Sicily. Fall of Mussolini.
	August	First Quebec Conference.
	September	Allied forces invaded Italian mainland.
	December	Teheran Conference.
1944	June	Invasion of Normandy.
	September	Second Quebec conference.
	October	Churchill and Eden visited Moscow.
1945	February	Yalta conference.
	April	Deaths of Roosevelt, Mussolini and Hitler. Truman became US President.
	May	Unconditional surrender by Germany.
	July	General Election. Labour victory. Clement Attlee became Prime Minister.
	July-August	Potsdam Conference.
	August	Atomic bomb dropped on Hiroshima and

		Nagasaki. Japan surrendered.
	December	American loan agreement.
1946	March	Churchill's Iron Curtain speech.
	July	Serious rioting in India.
	July	King David Hotel blown up in Jerusalem.
1947	February	Mountbatten made Viceroy of India.
	February	Britain told USA she could no longer aid Greece and Turkey.
	March	Truman Doctrine.
	June	Marshall Aid Plan announced.
	August	India and Pakistan granted independence.
	December	Britain announced it will quit Palestine.
1948	February	Communists seized power in Czechoslovakia.
	March	Brussels collective security treaty.
	April	OEEC set up.
	May	Britain withdrew from Palestine.
	June	Start of Berlin blockade.
1949	April	North Atlantic Treaty signed.
	May	Berlin blockade lifted.
	August	USSR tested its first atomic bomb.
	September	Sterling devalued.
	September	Mao-Tse-tung came to power in China.
1950	February	General Election. Narrow Labour victory.
	May/June	Britain declined to join ECSC.
	June	Start of Korean War.
	September	Labour government announced £3,600 million rearmament programme.
	October	Pleven Plan.
	November	China came to the aid of North Korea.
1951	March	Bevin retired. Morrison became Foreign Secretary.
	April	Anglo-Iranian Oil Company nationalised.
	October	General Election. Conservative victory. Winston Churchill became Prime Minister.
1952	October	First British atomic bomb tested.
1953	January	D.D.Eisenhower became US President.
	March	Death of Stalin.
	May	Churchill pressed for detente with Russia.
	July	End of Korean War.
	July	Churchill had a stroke.
	August	Mussadiq overthrown in Iran.
1954	May-July	Geneva Conference on Indo-China.
	July	Anglo-Egyptian treaty. Britain to withdraw from Suez base by 1956.

September	Britain joined South East Asia Treaty Organisation.
October	London Nine Power Agreement.
1955 April	Eden replaced Churchill as Prime Minister.
April	Britain joined Baghdad Pact.
May	General Election. Victory for Eden.
1956 June	Suez base evacuated.
July	Nasser nationalised Suez Canal Company.
Oct.-Nov.	Anglo-French expedition to Suez.
1957 January	Harold Macmillan replaced Eden as Prime Minister.
January	Defence White Paper emphasised nuclear deterrence and abolished National Service by 1960.
March	Treaty of Rome.
March	Ghana received independence.
May	Britain tested hydrogen bomb.
1958 July	British troops sent to defend Jordan.
November	Russian threat to West Berlin.
1959 February	Macmillan visited Moscow.
October	General Election. Conservative victory.
1960 January	EFTA in operation.
February	Macmillan's 'wind of change' speech.
June	Britain purchased Skybolt from the USA.
October	Monckton Report on Central African Federation.
December	Nigeria became independent.
1961 January	J.F.Kennedy became US President.
March	South Africa left the Commonwealth.
July	Cabinet agreed to apply for membership of EEC.
July	British task force sent to defend Kuwait.
August	Berlin Wall constructed.
1962 Oct.-Nov.	Cuban Missiles Crisis.
December	Macmillan had talks with de Gaulle.
December	Britain purchased Polaris from the USA.
1963 January	French veto on British application to join EEC.
June	Victoria Falls Conference arranged dissolution of Central African Federation.
August	Test Ban Treaty.
October	Sir Alexander Douglas-Home replaced Macmillan as Prime Minister.
November	Assassination of President Kennedy.
December	Central African Federation dissolved.
1964 October	General Election. Labour victory. Harold Wilson became Prime Minister.

Further Reading

You will not be surprised to learn that there are hundreds of excellent books on British foreign and imperial policy for this period. It is impossible for most students to consult more than just a few of these. However, it is vital that you read some, particularly if you are taking the period as a special or depth study. This period is one of considerable controversy and you will be in a better position to form your own conclusions if you have read widely. The following suggestions are meant to serve as a guide from which you might wish to 'pick and mix'.

1 Textbooks

There are many general works that cover all or most of this period and which examine domestic as well as foreign and imperial policy. Among the best are:

K.G. Robbins, *The Eclipse of a Great Power: Modern Britain 1870-1975* (Longman 1983)

A. Sked and C. Cook, *Post-War Britain* (Penguin 1984)

W.N. Medlicott, *Contemporary England* (Longman 1976). (This book, although a bit dated, is particularly strong on foreign policy.)

D. Childs, *Britain Since 1945* (Methuen 1986)

K.O. Morgan, *The People's Peace. British History 1945-1989* (Oxford University Press 1990)

2 General texts on British Foreign Policy

The most accessible of the modern texts, giving up-to-date interpretations on many of the relevant issues, include:

D. Reynolds, *Britannia Overruled: British Policy and World Power in the Twentieth Century* (Longman 1991)

R. Douglas, *World Crisis and British Decline, 1929-56* (Macmillan 1986)

C.J. Bartlett, *British Foreign Policy in the Twentieth Century* (Macmillan 1989)

R. Holland, T*he Pursuit of Greatness. Britain and the World Role, 1900-1970* (Fontana 1991)

All these books examine British foreign policy over slightly different periods. All try to account for Britain's (relative) decline. Reynolds is particularly worth reading. His book, which covers British policy throughout the 20th century, will enable you to view the events of 1939-64 in a wider context.

3 Anglo-American Relations

Some books concentrate on Anglo-American relations. Among the best are:

D. Dimbleby and D. Reynolds, *An Ocean Apart* (Hodder and Stoughton 1988) - a readable and scholarly text which examines the growth of the special relationship this century. It is best read in conjunction with the TV series which it was produced to accompany. (Your school/college/university may have video copies.)
C.J. Bartlett, *The Special Relationship. A Political History of Anglo-American Relations since 1945* (Longman 1992) is more recent.

4 General Texts on British Imperial Policy
Numerous books discuss Britain's relations with her colonies and with the Commonwealth. Among the best are:
T.O. Lloyd, *The British Empire 1558-1983* (Oxford University 1984) - you only need to read the last few chapters.
J.G. Darwin, *Britain and Decolonisation* (Macmillan 1988) - a perceptive and persuasive text, well worth reading from cover to cover.
J.G. Darwin, *The End of the British Empire: The Historical Debate* (Blackwell 1991) - a short and interesting read, especially for those who have already established the 'shape' of the topic in their minds.
B. Lapping, *The End of Empire* (Granada 1985) is based on a TV series and provides a detailed narrative of events in Britain's main colonies.

5 The Second World War
Excellent and reasonably short-ish accounts of the war include:
M. Kitchen, *A World in Flames* (Longman 1990)
A.J.P. Taylor, *The Second World War: an Illustrated History* (Penguin 1975)
P. Calvocoressi and G Wint, *Total War* (Penguin 1972) is a good read and you should not be put off by its length! Winston Churchill's own work, *The Second World War* 6 vols (Cassell 1948-54) will probably be too long for most students but remains worth dipping into.

Churchill has been the subject of many excellent biographies. These include:
H. Pelling, *Winston Churchill* (Macmillan 1974)
M. Gilbert, *Churchill. A Life* (Heinemann 1991)
J. Charmley, *The End of Glory* (1992 Hodder and Stoughton) which raises considerable doubts about Churchill's war record.

6 Labour Foreign Policy
P. Hennessy, *Never Again. Britain 1945-1951* (Cape 1992) is sweeping in scope, highly readable and penetrating in analysis. Read it!
Two biographies are also worth reading or sampling:
K. Harris, *Attlee* (Weidenfeld and Nicolson 1982)
A. Bullock, *Ernest Bevin, Foreign Secretary* (Heinemann 1983) - a

massive work, full of important information as well as providing a convincing portrait of this most important Foreign Secretary.
Two collections of essays also worth attention:
R. Ovendale (Ed), *Foreign Policy of the British Labour Governments 1945-51* (Leicester University 1984)
M. Dockrill and J.W. Young (Eds), *British Foreign Policy 1945-56* (Macmillan 1989) - also useful for Churchill and Eden's foreign policy.

7 Churchill and Eden (1951-55)

Perhaps the best work on this period is **A. Seldon,** *Churchill's Indian Summer. The Conservative Government 1951-55* (Hodder and Stoughton 1981) - convincingly pro-Churchill!
J.W. Young (Ed), *The Foreign Policy of Churchill's Peacetime Administration 1951-1955* (Leicester University 1988) - a valuable collection of essays, some of which are critical of Churchill.
M. Gilbert, *Never Despair. Winston Churchill, 1945-1965* (Heinemann 1988) - the last volume in Gilbert's epic biography.

8. Eden and Suez

The best works on Anthony Eden and Suez include:
R. Rhodes James, *Anthony Eden* (Weidenfeld and Nicolson 1986) - a sympathetic 'official' biography based largely on Eden's papers.
D. Carlton, *Anthony Eden. A Biography* (Allen Lane 1981) - far more critical of Eden.
H. Thomas, *The Suez Affair* (Weidenfeld & Nicolson 1986) - originally published in 1966 but still a key text.
Wm.R. Louis and R. Owen (Eds), *Suez 1956. The Crisis and its Consequences* (Clarendon 1989) - an interesting collection of essays.
K. Kyle, *Suez* (Weidenfeld and Nicolson 1991) - makes use of more recent material and, although long, is very readable.

9 Harold Macmillan (1957-63)

The best book (by far) is: **A. Horne,** *Macmillan,* Vol II 1957-1986 (Macmillan 1989). This will give you a superb feel of both the man and the period. H. Macmillan's own three volumes, *Riding the Storm, 1956-59* (Macmillan 1971), *Pointing the Way 1959-1961* (Macmillan 1973), and *At the End of the Day 1961-1963* (Macmillan 1975) remain a very rich source of material.

10 More Specialist Works

Students who wish to track down more specialist works can most effectively start via the bibliographies in Reynolds' (1991) volume.

Index